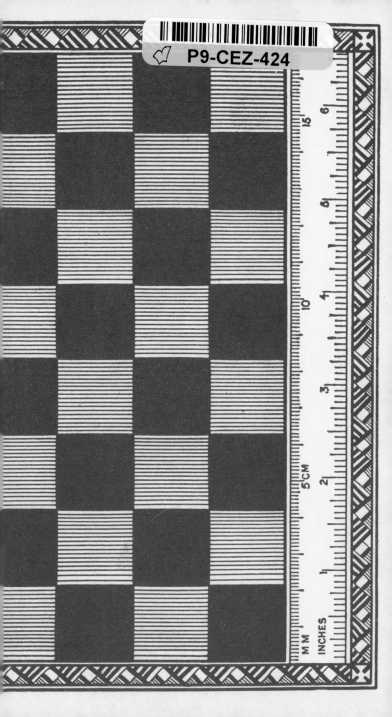

THE WEEK-END PROBLEMS BOOK

THE
WEEK-END
PROBLEMS
BOOK

COMPILED BY
HUBERT PHILLIPS
alias "Caliban" of the NEW STATESMAN;
alias "Dogberry" of the NEWS–CHRONICLE;
Composer of "Trinculo's" Crosswords

A Nonesuch book
published by
Duckworth Overlook
London · New York · Woodstock

This edition published in 2006 by
Duckworth Overlook
in association with The Nonesuch Press

LONDON
90-93 Cowcross Street
London EC1M 6BF
inquiries@duckworth-publishers.co.uk
www.ducknet.co.uk

WOODSTOCK
The Overlook Press
One Overlook Drive
Woodstock, NY 12498
www.overlookpress.com
[for individual orders and bulk sales in the United States,
please contact our Woodstock office]

NEW YORK
The Overlook Press
141 Wooster Street
New York, NY 10012

Every effort has been made to trace all copyright holders,
but if any have been overlooked, the publisher
will be pleased to make the necessary arrangements
at the first opportunity.

A CIP catalogue record for this book is available
from the British Library

ISBN 0 7156 3533 6 (UK)
ISBN 1-58567-858-9 (US)

Typeset by Ray Davies
Printed in Great Britain by
Creative Print and Design Ltd, Ebbw Vale

FOREWORD

In presenting the *Week-End Problems Book* to the public, I have pleasure in making the following acknowledgements.

First, to the *New Statesman and Nation*, in which the great majority of the "Caliban" problems have been published, as well as "Trinculo's" Crosswords; and to the *News-Chronicle*, in which have appeared (in "Dogberry's" column) most of the "Time Tests of Intelligence" and a few of the miscellaneous Word Puzzles. The friendly interest shown by readers of these journals has been a source of continued encouragement.

Next, to Mr Ely Culbertson and his (and my) publishers, Messrs Faber and Faber, for permission to make use of Contract Bridge material. On the technique of Contract, Mr Culbertson speaks with unrivalled authority, and his co-operation has added greatly to the value of the book.

Not less valuable has been Mr Comins Mansfield's help in the selection and editing of the Chess Problems. It will be generally agreed, I think, that Mr Mansfield has brought together the most brilliant collection of problems ever assembled in so small a compass.

I have also to thank Lord Dunsany for permission to include his "Inferential" Problems. These will prove a source of delight to many.

A number of friends have assisted in the reading and correction of proof sheets, and have made constructive suggestions of various kinds. I have to thank, in particular, Dr L.C. Adam, Miss Margaret Phillips, Wing-Commander Struan Marshall, and Messrs. F.G.B. Atkinson, D. Barber, W.J. Hodgetts, H. Kempson, G.P. Meredith, W. Oldham, C.W. Roberts, S.T. Shovelton, and C.H. Waddington. I have had to reject, for technical reasons, a number of excellent ideas which they have contributed while the book was passing through the press; but further editions, should such be called for, will benefit even more from their good offices.

My wife is responsible for the selection of the Crosswords; "Trinculo" has no more assiduous solver or more devastating critic.

Finally, I must thank Mr Francis Meynell, of the *Nonesuch Press*, and Mr Walter Lewis and his staff of Readers, for the care and skill which they have given to a book the production of which itself set many a typographical problem.

HUBERT PHILLIPS
Nov. 1932.

CONTENTS

CONTENTS

CONTENTS

INTRODUCTION
TO THE 2006 EDITION

A single man fills his pipe and sets out a chess board. He 'parades the pieces' and inspects them for 'French shaves and loose buttons', before playing out the moves of a championship game between Gortchakoff and Meninkin. Who is he? Perhaps you know the answer already. He is Philip Marlowe, the chess playing hero of Raymond Chandler's novels. This particular scene happens in *The Long Goodbye* and Chandler uses it to deliver his verdict on what we might think of as the human condition. The game goes 'seventy-two moves to a draw, a prize specimen of the irresistible force meeting the immovable object, a battle without armour, a war without blood, and as elaborate a waste of human intelligence as you could find outside an advertising agency'.

So many windmills, so little time to tilt! And yet for all his implied disdain for the game and its protagonists, Marlowe cannot resist. In *The High Window*, during yet another bout of whiskey, chess and introspection, he plays a game by the great José Raúl Capablanca. 'It went fifty-nine moves. Beautiful, cold, remorseless chess, almost creepy in its silent implacability.'

Back to *The Long Goodbye*. Here Marlowe lays out a problem known as 'The Sphinx', the solution of which requires a full eleven moves. Chess problems usually require four or five moves from the solver. 'An eleven mover is sheer unadulterated torture,' Marlowe says. 'Once in a while when I feel mean enough I set it out and look for a new way to solve it. It's a nice quiet way to go crazy.'

Welcome, then, to *The Week-End Problems Book*, as fine a collection of puzzles as I have met and a genial invitation either to go crazy or, if you prefer, elaborately to waste

1

your intelligence without first getting a job in an advertising agency.

It was first published by Hubert Phillips in 1932, during what we might regard as the heyday of puzzles and problems. This was a time before television and Phillips, like many of his contemporaries, was a prolific author of epigrams, puzzles and satirical verse. For sixteen years he was the crossword editor of the *News Chronicle* and his satirical column, 'Dogberry', ran in the same publication for over twenty years. In the *New Statesman,* he set famously devilish puzzles under the pseudonym 'Caliban'. Later in the decade he would go on to captain the England bridge team. To this day mixed teams-of-four compete for the English Bridge Union's Hubert Phillips Bowl. His puzzles expected of his audience a certain erudition – he read history and economics at Oxford – but also wit, charm, enthusiasm and, above all, a sense of humour. By all accounts he was a genial man, the perfect companion for a long evening of self-made entertainment, and in this sense he was very much a man of his time. Among his many publications are *Caliban's Problem Book, The Complete Book of Card Games,* the Penguin *Hoyle* and *Brush Up Your Wits*. He also published over a hundred crime-problem stories and a novel, *Charteris Royal. The Week-End Problems Book* represents the best of this multi-talented man.

Some of the games – chess, for example – had been around a long time. But others were new. In early 1932 contract bridge was less than seven years old, having been created by Harold 'Mike' Vanderbilt whilst on a cruise through the Panama Canal on 31st October 1925. At this time crosswords were still in their infancy. It was only in the previous year that the *Times* had, in response to public demand, started running a puzzle. This was quite a turnaround. Seven years earlier the same paper had declared that, 'All America has succumbed to the crossword puzzle,' which it claimed was 'a menace because it is making devastating inroads on the working hours of every rank and society'. By way of corroboration, its New York correspondent estimated in 1924 that Americans spent five million hours every day doing crossword puzzles, and that many of these hours should in fact have been spent working.

But Queen Mary and Stanley Baldwin were early converts to crosswords, as were millions of newspaper readers, and, by 1931, all British daily papers carried a crossword. The first *Times* setter was a farmer called Adrian Bell. I remember once interviewing his daughter, Anthea, about what it was like to live with a man whose job it was to tease, frustrate and delight the nation over their breakfast toast. She recalled that her father always said the point was not to make the solver chuckle. The point was to 'make him groan, preferably with satisfaction'. Bell would test clues out on his children at breakfast. 'Die of cold? (3,4)'1 came to her mind as we spoke.

1931 was also the year in which the game of bridge became a global phenomenon, largely through the efforts of Ely Culbertson, whose bridge problems are included in this book. His biographer, John Clay, rightly calls him 'the man who made contract bridge', but it is Culbertson's shifting assessment of the game that holds our attention. He first encountered it on a transatlantic crossing when he stopped to watch a four playing. They urged him to join them, which he did. But he was no good at it, recalling in his memoirs that, 'After a few sessions I gave up in disgust. *It's a stupid game*, I thought.' A year later he was reintroduced to the game by 'a girl' whose parents were 'rich enough to send her to one of those foreign schools where, in a mere two years, a perfectly nice girl is usually turned into a finished product of useless knowledge and imitation glamour.' Part of which, even then, was a working (though possibly useless) knowledge of bridge. Again he was not impressed. But a decade later he had made

* ICE CUBE

the game his own, and, by way of introduction to yet another bestseller, described it like this: 'Simple enough for a grown-up child and yet deep enough for a demigod, it has this in common with the strategy of actual warfare; the side that makes the fewer blunders is victorious.'

Which brings us back to *The Week-End Problems Book*, and its world of chess and bridge, of word games and crossword puzzles, of logic and frustration. Simple enough for children, yet deep enough for demigods. Or even, gentle reader, you. The intellectual challenges are intended as much to frustrate as to delight. As much but not more so. These competing emotions are meant to be there in equal measure. Their combined effect is Adrian Bell's 'groan of satisfaction'. I once asked an eminent crossword setter how he approached his work and I am fond of his answer. 'A crossword setter,' he said, 'is entering a game in which the point is to lose gracefully.' Hubert Phillips, in his introduction to the original volume, says that his guiding principle is 'to provide the maximum amount of entertainment', which is essentially the same thing, for we are entertained, properly entertained, only when delight succeeds – though does not necessarily exceed – frustration.

And the point for the solver? It is the same, only different. The solver, by implication, must win, but he too must do it gracefully. Victory – another name for delight – is the aim, but victory over whom, or against what? For Philip Marlowe the victory is more than just the solution to a chess problem. His victory is the assertion of who he is, of his values and his story. His victory is also the escape, however temporary, into a cleaner, better world. A world of heroes. A world where the qualities he admires in life find their perfect expression on the chess board. My father's preference was the bridge table, which for much the same reasons, he referred to as his 'square yard of freedom'. And the freedom – in a definition of which one imagines Roosevelt would have approved – was as much 'from' as 'to'. It was the freedom from distraction, from chaos, from noise. It was the freedom to excel or to be cold, or implacable, or romantic, or heroic. It was the freedom to be at the centre of his own perfect world.

Chess and bridge, of course, are much akin, and their problems create the same response. Speaking of The Sphinx's eleven-mover, Philip Marlowe said, 'You don't even scream, but you come awfully close.' And, writing fifty years later, the great bridge player Zia Mahmood said, 'At bridge, no one can hear you scream.' This need not be true of *The Week-End Problems Book*. Share it with your friends and family; let them hear you scream. But share with them also your delight when sometimes, just sometimes, the compilers gracefully lose, and your victory is complete.

As to the question of victory over what? I suspect *that* is a puzzle only you can solve.

Sandy Balfour
January 2006

INTRODUCTION
TO THE PROBLEMS

In selecting the contents of this book of problems I have tried
to bear in mind two guiding principles: first, to provide the
maximum amount of entertainment; secondly, to avoid the
representation of problems which are already familiar. Except
in the Chess and Bridge sections (where my aim has been to
open up to non-specialists these two fascinating fields) most
of what I have published is quite new.

The book falls into four parts:

(i) Problems pure and simple, their solution depending in
the main on the application of logical and mathematical
principles.

(ii) Word puzzles of various types.

(iii) Chess problems.

(iv) Contract Bridge problems.

Readers will, I think, be interested in knowing what my
bases of selection have been.

(i)

Logical and Mathematical problems. The "Caliban" problems,
which are here offered as the reader's staple diet, are preceded
by a few *hors-d'oeuvre* called Time Tests of Intelligence. The
essence of these latter is that they should be done *quickly*, as
none of them is of great intrinsic difficulty. I have not specified
exactly how long should be allowed for the solution of each
problem, but few of them, I think, should take longer than
five minutes. The exceptions are one or two arithmetical
puzzles for which more time would be required by solvers
who do not calculate quickly.

Turning to the "Caliban" problems, I regard these as the

main (though by no means the only) justification of the book. These problems are, with one or two exceptions, original, and most of them have appeared in the "Playtime" column of the *New Statesman and Nation*. I am under a debt of gratitude to readers of that column, whose suggestions and friendly criticism have been of great encouragement in the formulation of these problems.

The "Caliban" problems can be classified (in the manner of Polonius) under the following five headings:

> (1) Inferential.
> (2) Inferential-factual.
> (3) Mathematical.
> (4) Inferential–mathematical.
> (5) Cryptographic.

Examples of these five classes are: of (1) *The Six Authors and Dogs*; of (2) *Dr Zbysco* and *Footprints in the Snow*; of (3) *The Mad Millionaires* and *Cubicles*; of (4) *Plutocrats at Play* and *Fun on the 'Phlegmatic'*; of (5) *Puschowski* and *E Tenebris Lux*. The widespread interest which, I am glad to think, obtains in my *New Statesman* column, is due, I imagine, to the wide range of intellectual weapons which the solving of these different types of problem brings into play.

The most popular of these problems are undoubtedly the purely *inferential ones* (Class 1). This is partly because they demand no mathematical technique, and partly because they can easily be made amusing; there is a keen pleasure in the logical sorting out of what seem to be hopelessly tangled relationships. On the other hand, these problems tend to exhibit a certain sameness, and it is rather a defect in them that they can be solved by guess–work; though little satisfaction can be derived from getting at the answer in this way.

Inferential-factual problems (Class 2) have proved themselves less satisfactory for *e.g.* competitive purposes; they have often led, when set in competitions, to protracted argument. This is because the data necessary to the solving of them include the individual judgements of the solver as to what is possible in real life and what is not. For example, in framing the much discussed problem of *Dr Zbysco's Murder*, I assumed that it was impossible for anyone to pass from a moving train to another train moving in the opposite direction; but one or two of my critics (admittedly a small minority) have maintained that such an occurrence is more likely than that which I actually envisaged. Hence, to make these problems fool-proof, one would want to set them out at much greater length, and this would necessitate further "padding" lest the solution should be spotted too easily. In short, the inferential-factual problem is an attempt to boil down a detective story and has the defects of this quality. From the point of view of entertainment, however – or so my experience suggests to me – they give as much pleasure as any.

"Straight" *mathematical* problems (Class 3) are naturally only of interest to those who are technically equipped to solve them. For that reason I have only included two or three. Mathematicians take a keen delight in *e.g.* applications of probability and in such problems as that of the *Cubicles*, and I think that in so comprehensive an anthology something should be done to meet their special tastes.

Inferential-mathematical problems (Class 4) are, in my opinion, the most attractive of all. The mathematics required are simple, so that these problems are not open to the objection that the non-expert cannot solve them; but they enable the application of strictly deductive methods to be varied and elaborated in all sorts of interesting ways. So far as I know, there will be found in this class several quite new types of problem. For example, *The Professor's Daughters*, *Fun on the 'Phlegmatic'*, and *Rain*, are different in type from one another, but all were quite fascinating puzzles to construct, and each opens up new possibilities that I shall hope presently to explore.

As for *cryptographs* (Class 5) I have nothing special to say.

This book is not intended for expert solvers of such things, and hence only quite elementary examples are included. Their solution necessarily depends primarily upon trial and error, and to that extent I think they are less interesting puzzles than other types.

(ii)

Word Puzzles. These are discussed on p. 103. I should, however, add that the Crosswords have all appeared in the *New Statesman and Nation*; that the Acrostics, in the main, have not been published before; and that the various other types of word puzzle, of which examples are given, have, in part, appeared in "Dogberry's" column in the *News Chronicle*. Perhaps the most interesting feature of this section is the collection of palindromic word squares. I am anxious to secure the co-operation of readers who may be interested in the working out of more satisfactory examples.

(iii)

Chess Problems. Here I would especially draw attention to Lord Dunsany's problems, which are quite different from the ordinary two or three mover. They are really studies in pure inference worked out through the medium of the chess board, and, as such, will be greatly appreciated by all solvers who like exercising their logical faculties and in addition know the rules of chess. Apart from Lord Dunsany's material, Mr Mansfield has brought together in this section the most brilliant collection of problems ever assembled in so small a compass.

(iv)

Contract Bridge Problems. Here I have ignored the familiar type of double dummy problem, since the best examples of these have appeared in print over and over again. Instead, problems of bidding and play are presented (based in part on Mr Ely

Culbertson's material, and in part on my own), which are not only comparatively fresh, but will serve in themselves as an introduction to modern Contract Bridge to those who are not well acquainted with its technique. These problems of bidding and play do not, of course, lend themselves to a unique solution, in the sense in which a chess problem does, but the answers given are – so far as such things can be – authoritative, and if some of them serve to stimulate inquiry and criticism, why, that is all to the good. I would draw attention also to the inclusion of a few studies in the new and fascinating game of Contract Whist.

TIME TESTS OF INTELLIGENCE

TIME TESTS OF INTELLIGENCE

• 1 •

A party of men went into a restaurant. Each gave exactly the same order and their total bill came to 6s. ¼d.

How many of them were there?

• 2 •

Two Americans entered the saloon bar of a public house.

One American was the father of the other American's son.

How is this to be explained?

• 3 •

A friend told me the following story:

"The Squire", she said, "died suddenly the other day. He and his wife went to church, and the day was very hot. The Squire fell asleep. He dreamed he was a French nobleman at the time of the Revolution. He had been condemned to be guillotined, and was waiting on the scaffold for the guillotine to fall.

"Just then his wife, noticing he was asleep, tapped him on the back of his neck with her fan. The shock was so great—in conjunction with his dream—that the Squire immediately died."

I said: "That story, on the face of it, is not true."

Why?

• 4 •

Ten counters, bearing the numbers 1 to 10 inclusive, were put into a bag. Henry, Alice, George, Mabel and Lucy drew out two counters each. The sum of the two numbers drawn in each case was: Henry, 16; Alice, 11; George, 4; Mabel, 17; Lucy, 7.

What, in each case, were the counters actually drawn?

• 5 •

"Two boys took up their station near the clock-tower to find out which could hold his breath the longer. Neither of them won; for the first boy held his breath from the first stroke of 12 to the sixth, and the other from the sixth stroke to the twelfth."

Some say this is an absurd statement, because you cannot count clock strokes while holding your breath; some, because the clock was probably late.

Do you think the statement absurd? and, if so, why?

• 6 •

Assume that the following statement is true: "John is over 21 if John can vote."

Which of the following statements are then necessarily *true also?*

(1) If John cannot vote, John is not over 21.

(2) If John is over 21, he can vote.

(3) If John is not over 21, he cannot vote.

(4) Either John can vote or John is not over 21.

(5) Either John cannot vote or he is over 21.

(6) Either John can vote or he is over 21.

(7) Either John cannot vote or he is not over 21.

• 7 •

Put three letters before the following and the same three letters in the same order after it, and so make a very familiar word:

ERGRO

• 8 •

"I have so built my house", writes Professor Popoff, "that the windows on all four sides face south."

How has the Professor contrived to do this?

14

• 9 •

Dad went up to town this afternoon with £1 in his pocket and came back with £3. He had bought a new hat at the hat-shop and some daffodils in the market place. He had also had a tooth stopped.

Dad gets paid on Friday and the banks are open on Tuesday, Thursday and Saturday.

The Dentist comes every day but Saturday.

Thursday is early closing day and there is no market on Friday.

What day of the week is it?

• 10 •

"The square on the hypot'nuse of a right-angled triangle", said Ptolemy to his sister, "is equal to the sum of the squares of the other two sides."

"Is that so?" said Ptopsy.

"It sure is", said Ptolemy.

"But s'pose it's an *equilat'ral* right-angled triangle—" said Ptopsy.

"A what?"

"—S'pose it's an *equilat'ral* right-angled triangle—"

"Yes."

"'Seems to me the hypot'nuse *can't* be bigger than the other sides; so what you say can't be true, Ptolemy."

"'Seems so", said Ptolemy, rubbing his nose. "P'raps there's an exception to the rule, Ptopsy."

Are they right in thinking so?

• 11 •

Swinging their tomahawks, the Big Indian and the Little Indian came striding down the road.

The Little Indian was the son of the Big Indian.

Yet the Big Indian was not the father of the Little Indian.

How is this to be explained?

• 12 •

A metal ingot weighs 13 pounds.

How can it be converted into three ingots, with which any number of pounds can be weighed from one to 13 inclusive?

• 13 •

Two schoolboys were playing on the toolshed roof. Something gave way, and they were precipitated, through the roof, on to the floor below.

When they picked themselves up, the face of one was covered with grime. The other's face was quite clean. Yet it was the boy with the clean face who at once went off and washed.

How is this to be explained?

• 14 •

One of the following three statements *must* be true:

(1) All Shakespeare's plays were written by Bacon.

(2) Some of Shakespeare's plays (but not all) were written by Bacon.

(3) Some of Shakespeare's plays were not written by Bacon.

We do not know which of these statements is true.

But—

Which pair of statements may both be true, but cannot both be false?

And—

Which pair of statements may both be false, but cannot both be true?

• 15 •

Negus and Co. sent Blotto a cheque for £100. The cheque was stolen in transit by Pinchem.

Pinchem forged Blotto's endorsement and took the cheque to a shop where he owed £50. He settled his debt with it and received the balance of £50 in cash.

Pinchem disappeared before the fraud had been discovered. The shop where he had settled his account was subsequently called on to refund to Negus and Co. the £100 for the cheque; it was then sent on to Blotto, the rightful owner.

How much money did the shop lose?

• 16 •

The following inscription was unearthed at Camulodunum (the Roman Colchester):

ORE STABIT FORTIS ARARE PLACET ORESTAT

Can you decipher it?

• 17 •

Mother went to the store to buy silk. The blue, the yellow, the red, the green, the brown and the mauve were each an exact number of shillings per yard, and no two were the same price.

Mother bought as many yards each of the blue, the red and the mauve as they respectively cost shillings per yard.

She received discount for cash at the rate of 2*d*. in the shilling, and was given change for a £5 note. Had she not received discount, £5 would not have been enough.

Had she bought the yellow, the green and the brown under the same conditions (i.e. as many yards of each as they respectively cost shillings per yard), she would have bought the same number of yards in all as she actually did buy; and would have spent the same amount as she actually spent.

How much did she spend?

• 18 •

What sum of money, expressed in pounds, shillings and pence, is expressed in farthings by the same digits in the same order? (For example, if the answer were £29.7*s*.1*d*. this would also be expressible as 2971 farthings.)

• 19 •

A pack of cards is well shuffled and divided into two equal packets. The top card of one packet is turned up, and is found to be a spade. The top card of the other packet is now turned up.

What are the chances that this is a spade?

• 20 •

Mr Cashbox, the millionaire, advertised for a financial adviser. Oof and Spoof were candidates. Mr Cashbox put to each of them the following question:

"Would you rather have £10,000 a year, rising by £2,000 annually, or £5,000 half-yearly, rising by £500 half-yearly?"

"The former", said Oof. "The latter", said Spoof.

Whom did Mr Cashbox engage, and why?

• 21 •

"That is my nephew", said George to his sister Georgina.

"He is not my nephew", said Georgina.

How is this to be explained?

• 22 •

All the trains from our station go to Fogwell. From Fogwell, some go on to Kemp; others, to Banstock and thence to Midvale; others, again, to Greenfields and on to Deane. The fare is ninepence to Kemp, Midvale or Deane; elsewhere, sixpence.

Father is in a hurry. He has taken a sixpenny ticket. The first train in was going to Midvale, but Father did not get in.

What is Father's destination?

• 23 •

Smith says his maid is unintelligent. He overheard this dialogue on the 'phone:

Voice: Is Mr Smith there?

Maid: I think so, Sir. What name, please?

Voice: Clew.

Maid: I beg pardon, Sir?

Voice: Clew. C for Crocodile, L for Lion, E for Elephant—

Maid: E for what, Sir?

Voice: E for Elephant, W for Walrus. C, L, E, W, Clew.

Maid: Thank you, Sir. I'll see if Mr Smith is in. ...

Why does Smith criticise his maid?

• 24 •

When I am as old as my father is now I shall be five times the age my son is now. By then my son will be eight years older than I am now. The combined ages of my father and myself total 100 years.

How old is my son?

• 25 •

Two vessels contained equal quantities of whisky and water. A teaspoonful of the whisky was transferred to the vessel containing water. A teaspoonful of the mixture from this vessel was then transferred to the vessel containing whisky.

How does the proportion of water in this vessel now compare with the proportion of whisky in the other?

• 26 •

Two men sold peaches. One sold small peaches at three for 1s., and he sold 30 every day, which brought him in 10s. The other sold larger peaches at two for 1s. and also sold 30 every day, which brought him in 15s. One day the first man arranged to sell all 60 peaches. As he sold the small ones at three for 1s. and the larger ones at two for 1s., he decided he

19

could dispose of the stock more quickly by selling five peaches for 2s.

At the end of the day he had sold all the peaches and had taken 24s. But 10s. and 15s. total 25s.

Where did the other shilling go?

• 27 •

Assuming that the following statements are *true*:

(1) All Americans are well-educated;

(2) Some Americans are teachers;

(3) Some teachers are not well-educated;

(4) All teachers are trained;

which of the following statements are necessarily *true also; and which are* necessarily *false?*

(5) Well-educated Americans are teachers;

(6) Well-educated teachers are American;

(7) American teachers are well-educated;

(8) Some teachers are not Americans;

(9) Some trained teachers are not well-educated;

(10) Well-educated teachers are not trained?

• 28 •

"As a result, presumably, of the increasing accessibility of the more subtle poisons, the proportion of undetected murders has risen from 17.2 per cent in 1920 to 37.9 per cent in 1930."

Do you see anything absurd in this statistical comparison?

• 29 •

A. "I have to pay a bill for 6½ *d*. with two coins, one of which must not be a sixpence."

B. (After profound thought.) "It can't be done, old chap."

A. "Oh, yes, it can."

Can it?

• 30 •

Four players at a bridge table played three rubbers at one shilling a hundred. Each of them had a different partner each rubber. The scores of the three rubbers were 800, 1300, and 1100 points.

One player won 10*s*.

What did the other three respectively lose or win?

• 31 •

Here are 12 incomplete sentences. Below are given, in a different order, the 12 words needed to complete them. See how quickly you can assign each of these 12 words to its appropriate sentence, on the assumption that all 12 words must be used:

(1) Locomotives have —.   (2) Some birds can —.
(3) New York is a —.   (4) Lilies are —.   (5) Forts have —.
(6) Motor cars use —.   (7) Snow is —.   (8) Steamships have —.   (9) Chicago is a —.   (10) Soldiers carry —.
(11) Clothes are cleaned with —.   (12) Airships can —.

The 12 words: *City, fly, guns, oil, flowers, whistles, propellers, sing, state, petrol, packs, white.*

• 32 •

The following is a straightforward statement, made confusing by the introduction of alternatives to some of its words and phrases. Cross out the phrases that are superfluous:

"On the first of July, 1927, I said:

'My brother who $\begin{cases} \text{was born} \\ \text{was married} \\ \text{died} \end{cases}$ on the 15th June $\begin{cases} 1888 \\ 1894 \\ 1899 \end{cases}$

$\begin{cases} \text{was} \\ \text{would have been} \\ \text{will be} \end{cases}$ $\begin{cases} \text{twenty-five} \\ \text{twenty-seven} \\ \text{twenty-nine} \end{cases}$ years old last $\begin{cases} \text{week} \\ \text{month} \\ \text{year} \end{cases}$'."

• 33 •

Below are given the names of a number of countries, but
with certain letters missing. The missing letters are indicated
by stars.

Can you, *within three minutes*, complete the name of each
country?

(1) ** N * D *	(6) ** L*V **
(2) * ND **	(7) * EX ***
(3) **YP *	(8) P ** S **
(4) * H ** A	(9) ** EE * E
(5) * H * L *	(10) ** R W *Y

• 34 •

"Among the passengers on the S.S. *Boracic*, which docked at
Plymouth yesterday, was Mr Denzil Wapentake. Mr Wapentake,
who has just concluded a successful tour of the leading
American cities, was—as usual—smoking a cigar with abandon
as he walked down the gangplank. He expressed his pleasure
at being in England again."

This paragraph gave great offence to Mr Wapentake.
Why?

• 35 •

A cricket team has two bowlers, Smith and Jones. Before
their last match, their averages are the same, and they have
taken 30 wickets between them. In the last match Smith takes
3 for 24 and Jones 2 for 26. Their averages for the season are
now worked out and are found in each case to be 4.

What are their respective figures for the season?

• 36 •

Chilidor and Parazil are two neighbouring American states.
Their currencies (dollars and cents) are regarded as inter-
changeable. Owing to a trading dispute, however, the
Chilidor Government enacts that within its frontiers the

Parazil dollar shall be worth only 90 cents. The Parazil Government similarly depreciates the dollar of Chilidor. At the frontier town of Sezú in Parazil, a traveller buys 10 cents' worth of wine at an estaminet. He tenders a Parazil dollar, and receives a Chilidor dollar in exchange. He crosses the frontier, and buys a second drink at an estaminet in Chilidor, receiving this time a Parazil dollar. He continues to do this till he cannot tell one dollar from another.

Who pays for the traveller's drinks?

• 37 •

The Queen of Ruritania went shopping with her younger sister. Each bought as many lengths of silk as she is years old; and as many yards of each length as she had bought lengths; and paid for it as many francs per yard as she had bought yards of each length.

The Queen spent 5803 francs more than her sister.

How old is the Queen?

• 38 •

Two cyclists, John and George, start simultaneously from two points, A and B, 60 miles apart, to cycle towards one another along a straight road. John goes at 10 m.p.h. and George at 15 m.p.h. A fly, travelling at 20 m.p.h., leaves point A at the same time as John, and flies along the road till he meets George; when he turns about and flies back again to John. He proceeds thus to fly back and forth until the two cyclists meet.

What distance has the fly then covered?

• 39 •

A train is controlled by an engine-driver, a fireman and a guard, whose names are Brown, Jones and Robinson, *not* respectively.

On the train are three passengers: Mr Jones, Mr Robinson and Mr Brown.

Mr Robinson lives at Leeds.

The guard lives halfway between Leeds and London.

Mr Jones' income is £400. 2*s*.1*d*. per annum.

The guard earns in a year exactly one-third of the income of his nearest neighbour who is a passenger.

The guard's namesake lives in London.

Brown beat the fireman at billiards.

What is the name of the engine-driver?

• 40 •

Miss Green is the headmistress of a small school, which has never had more than 200 pupils. Every year she is given an allowance for equipment. This is calculated according to the following simple formula: for every girl in the school Miss Green gets as many pennies to spend as there are girls to spend them on.

This year Miss Green has been given £13.17*s*.7*d*. more than last year.

How many girls are there in the school?

• 41 •

"We'd a terrible time getting here", writes Sir George. "I had with me the four natives, Sambo, Jumbo, Tembo and Limbo. I could not leave Jumbo with either Sambo or Tembo, or Tembo with Limbo. Our canoe only holds two, and Sambo and I are the only ones who can handle it. Limbo, moreover, refused to be one of the first to cross.

"Imagine the time we had crossing the Limpopo, and the number of journeys we had to make."

How did Sir George get his party across?

THE "CALIBAN"
PROBLEMS

THE "CALIBAN" PROBLEMS

• 1 •

SLOCOMBE'S BANK

A forged cheque was presented at Slocombe's Bank about 3 p.m. on Thursday. It is certain that it was presented by one of the following: Pickler, Larkins and Dubb.

The police took the following statements:

From Pickler: I admit I was in the Bank on Thursday. I remember speaking to Dubb. I did not present any cheque. I should think the guilty man is Larkins.

From Larkins: I was not in the Bank on Thursday. Dubb is innocent. Pickler has never spoken to him in his life. Of course, Dubb is badly in need of money.

From Dubb: I was in the Bank about 3 on Thursday. Pickler certainly did not speak to me. I did not present the forged cheque. I am not in any need of money.

Each of these statements contains four assertions, and in each case three assertions, and three only, are in actual fact true.

Who presented the forged cheque?

• 2 •

PAUL'S CHRISTMAS PRESENTS

The Rector has seven daughters: Ada, Beryl, Clara, Dorothy, Evelyn, Francis and Grace.

Christmas presents are sent by each of them to one or more of the same seven young men.

Ada sends the greatest number of presents; Beryl the next greatest number; Grace the smallest number.

Paul receives the greatest number of presents; George the next greatest number; Richard the smallest number.

It is known that George, Henry, Albert and James receive presents from Ada; that George, Henry and Charles receive presents from Beryl; and that Charles and James receive presents from Clara.

Seventeen presents are sent in all.

From which of the seven girls does Paul receive them?

• 3 •

UNITED v. VILLA

Four teams—the Arsenal, the Hotspur, the United and the Villa—take part in an Association football competition. Each team plays each of the others once. Two points are awarded for a win and one for a draw.

The United score 5 points; the Hotspur, 3 points; the Villa, 1 point. Thirteen goals are scored in all, seven of these by the Hotspur; the Arsenal score no goals at all.

The Hotspur beat the Villa by 4 goals to 1.

What was the score in the game between the Villa and the United?

• 4 •

THE BLUE AND RED BALLS

The Professor had five blue balls in Bag No. 1. He transferred one of them to Bag No. 2, containing red balls. He drew a ball from this bag at random and transferred it to Bag No. 1. Finally he transferred a ball drawn at random from Bag No. 1 to Bag No. 2.

If he now draws a ball from Bag No. 2, the chances that it is a red one are 3—2.

How many red balls were there in Bag No. 2 originally?

• 5 •

A MILLIONAIRE GIVES ORDERS

Guggelheim, the Pittsburg millionaire, sent for a radio form when halfway across the Atlantic. He wrote out the following message, which he handed to me:

SARAD	EARBO	LDGIR	LTOWN
GOODW	IDEAR	EAYOU	RESAU
KEEPE	RICRA	TSBEA	RCATS
ROLLY	ARNOM	ENBOY	SMOTH
EVENS	LIMPO	LLMUF	FIVOR
PRAYD	EEMCO	RASLO	WABLE
KEEPD	OGSTO	WNNOT	EPAST
WITHO	GREPL	AYMAD	ENISI
NEARA	GUEMO	STXYZ	

It was addressed to his agents on Wall Street. "I should think the secret would be out in about ten minutes", said I.

"Long enough for my purposes", said Guggelheim. "I can't be bothered to put the message in cipher."

What is Guggelheim's message?

• 6 •

DOGS

In our village there are seven residents whose names are Mr Bloodhound, Mr Cocker, Mr Mastiff, Mr Peke, Mr Pom, Mr Pug and Mr St Bernard.

They severally, but not respectively, possess a bloodhound, a cocker, a mastiff, a peke, a pom, a pug, and a St Bernard.

None of them has a dog of a breed of the same name as himself.

Three of the villagers have dogs which are considerably larger than these villagers' canine namesakes.

Mr Mastiff's dog's human namesake is married.

The St Bernard's owner is Mr Pom's wife's sister's husband.

The mastiff weighs the same as his owner's fiancée.

Mr St Bernard's dog's human namesake is the owner of the peke.

The cocker's owner's canine namesake is owned by the human namesake of Mr Mastiff's dog.

Of the seven villagers, Mr Peke and Mr Pug are the only bachelors.

Which dog belongs to whom?

• 7 •

WHO KILLED POPOFF?

Popoff was murdered in the train between Badminster and Clew.

The train left Badminster at 10 a.m., arrived Clew 10.55 a.m., left Clew 11 a.m., and reached Drayton 11.20 a.m.

It is 40 miles from Badminster to Clew; 10 from Clew to Drayton, and the line is a perfectly straight one.

Hopkins and Watt are implicated.

Hopkins lives at Alehouse, 50 miles (in a straight line) from Badminster and 32 (in a straight line) from Drayton. (There is also a direct road from Alehouse to Clew.) He left Alehouse on his bicycle at 5.10 a.m. and returned at 2 p.m.

Watt lives at Clew. His car was in the garage until 8.10 a.m. at least. At 9.40 a.m. Watt was seen outside the garage in the car, which was back in the garage for good by 11.35 a.m.

Watt left the train at Drayton and was seen in Clew at 12.30 p.m.

The maximum speed of the car is 60 m.p.h.; of the bicycle 10 m.p.h. Hopkins cannot drive a car.

What were the movements of Hopkins and Watt, and who killed Popoff?

· 8 ·

THE RURITANIAN CABINET

The Ruritanian Cabinet has voted on a number of issues.

"Nevertheless", said the Prime Minister to the King, "on every issue the Government has a clear majority.

"I am the only Minister, however, who voted with the majority on each of the issues raised."

"What was the attitude of other Ministers?" asked the King.

The Prime Minister consulted his notes.

"The Minister for War", he said, "on eight occasions voted with the minority. The Lord Chancellor on seven occasions. The Postmaster General and the Minister for Air on five occasions each. The Home Secretary, the Governor of the Bank, and the Clerk of the Weather on three occasions each. And every other member of the Cabinet on one occasion only."

"Odd", said the King.

"I can tell your Majesty something still odder", said the Prime Minister. "On each contentious issue every member of the Cabinet voted; the majority was not the same on any two issues: and we achieved every possible distribution of votes, as between the majority and the minority."

How many Ministers are there in the Ruritanian Cabinet?

· 9 ·

INTERROGATORY

A burglary is committed in West Kensington on the night of Thursday, February 9th. It is known to be a one-man job. The only "clues" left by the burglar are a pair of gloves, a jemmy and a dark lantern.

The police at once detain five men on suspicion: Jukes (known as "Piggy"), Puddock, Sniffwell, Kickshaw, and Titterdown. Inspector Snooper asks permission from the Commissioner to interrogate these suspects.

The Commissioner, in view of criticism in the press, is a little nervous. He finally agrees, however, that the following four questions shall be put to each of the men detained. No other question may be asked:

(1) Where were you on the Thursday night?

(2) When were you last in West Kensington?

(3) What do you know about (here are named the four men other than the one under interrogation)?

(4) Have you ever possessed housebreaking implements?

The following are the answers to these questions (they are not answered on oath; the men are all of bad character; and hence it is not to be assumed that any answer is necessarily true):

Jukes: I spent Thursday night at the *Dog and Duck*. I have never been anywhere near Kensington. Titterdown is the man you're looking for; he always carries a jemmy. I never do.

Puddock: Me and Piggy went on the spree. Both of us is as white as they make 'em. I wouldn't be seen dead in Kensington either with housebreaking implements or without.

Sniffwell: I was in bed Thursday—I've got the arthritis something awful. Puddock knows Kensington best; he's got the tools for the job too. That was his lantern wot you found there.

Kickshaw: I was down Hammersmith way all right, if you call that West Kensington. But so was Puddock. I lent him a jemmy a week or two ago.

Titterdown: Thursday I took my Kate to see the pictures. We came through Kensington on the way home. I've never had no illegal tools of any kind: if I wanted any, I should borrow them from Jim Paddock.

On the strength of these statements, one of the five suspects is arrested by Inspector Snooper.

Whom does he arrest?

• 10 •

THE SCHOOLGIRL'S CIPHER

Message intercepted by Miss Frogmore, form-mistress of the Upper IV, during a geography lesson:

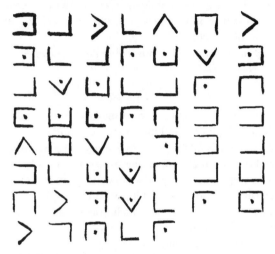

What did Miss Frogmore make of it?

• 11 •

THE NINE DINERS

"I won't sit next to Jones", said Robinson at the dinner-table. "Nor I next to Mrs Smith", said Mrs Brown. Jones' wife sat two places to his left; Brown had two ladies on each side of him; Robinson sat next-but-one to his wife, and Smith next-but-two to Miss Jones. Mrs Jones sat between her son and daughter, and Mrs Robinson between two men.

Show how the nine diners were seated, beginning with any one of them and going clockwise round the table.

• 12 •

THE FIVE RED BALLS

The Professor has a number of balls of various colours. He put a certain number (the colours of which were not known) in a bag, and the class then drew out five at random. All five were red.

"That that would happen", said the Professor, "was exactly an even money chance."

How many balls in all had he put in the bag, and how many of them were red ones?

• 13 •

BETTER THAN BOGEY

Spooph was going round the course at St Andwich. "I'll do a deal with you," said Ooph. "If you'll pay me £5 in respect of every hole at which you're one stroke down on bogey; and £10 in respect of every hole at which you're two strokes down on bogey and so on, I'll pay you £6, £12, and so on, in respect of every hole at which you're one, two or more strokes up on bogey."

"Done!" said Spooph.

He went round the course in 73. In respect of no hole was he more than two strokes down on bogey, or better than two strokes up. He was "all square" with bogey at each of the first three holes, but did not square another one till he reached the 11th. Ooph paid him £25.

What is bogey for the St Andwich course?

• 14 •

THE ACE OF SPADES

I have three packs of playing cards with identical backs. Let me call them packs A, B and C.

I draw a card at random from pack A and shuffle it in with pack B.

I now turn up the top card of pack A and find it is the Queen of Hearts.

Next, I draw a card at random from pack B and shuffle it in with pack C. Then, turning up the top card of pack B, I find that that is the Queen of Hearts also.

I now draw a card at random from pack C and place it at the bottom of pack A.

What is the chance that the top card of pack C is now the Ace of Spades?

· 15 ·

"E TENEBRIS LUX"

The "international crook" Xylonides was found in possession of the following crudely-drawn diagram.

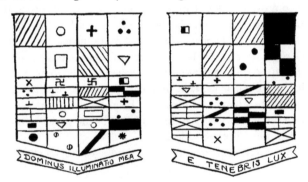

What did Scotland Yard make of it?

· 16 ·

MURDER OF DR ZBYSCO

Dr Zbysco left Addleville by the night train to town, departing from Addleville at 10.40 p.m. The train reached Botherham at 11.08 p.m., left at 11.10 p.m. and arrived punctually at Clutter at 11.29 p.m. It left Clutter at 11.34 p.m. and reached Didham at 12.14 a.m. next morning.

Dr Zbysco presented his ticket for inspection between Addleville and Botherham.

At Didham Dr Zbysco was found stabbed in an otherwise empty compartment. There was no trace of a struggle.

It can be taken for granted that the murderer was Pocombe, Borer, or Pusch.

Pocombe entered the train at Addleville. He occupied a compartment with eight other travellers, all of whom swear he never left it until the train was about to stop at Clutter. He then went out "to buy papers".

Borer lives at Eazle, some thirty miles from Botherham. He booked for Didham at Botherham station at 11.05 p.m., but stopped so long in the booking office, chatting to the booking-clerk, that he failed to catch the train. He can prove that he at once drove to Clutter in his car, and must have boarded the train there; as he certainly alighted from it at Didham.

Pusch lives at Didham. He booked for Botherham at Didham station at 10.13 p.m. His train reached Clutter at 10.52 p.m. and left at 10.56 p.m., and the guard and collector are prepared to swear that he was still on the train. It reached Botherham at 11.16 p.m.

Dr Zbysco when found had been dead for "at least an hour". For this we have the evidence of the police surgeon and another quite reliable doctor.

In what circumstances, and by whom, was Dr Zbysco murdered?

• 17 •

MATES

At the Lvov Chess Tournament in 19— there were ten competitors, each of whom played each of the others once. One point was awarded for a win and half a point for a draw. The competitors finished in the following order:

1. Casabianca	6. Morfew
2. Alasker	7. Snooper
3. Steinisch	8. Algonquin
4. Spilsbury	9. Titterdown
5. M'Bang M'Wang	10. Puschowski

Puschowski drew four of his games. Five competitors did not

lose a game at all. No one fared worse, against any particular competitor, than any competitor placed lower in the final table.

What was the result of the games (1) *between Alasker and Snooper;* (2) *between Steinisch and Morfew;* (3) *between Casabianca and M'Bang M'Wang?*

· 18 ·
THE UTOPIAN LEAGUE

Six teams are entered for the Utopian League championship. Each plays each of the others once. Two points are awarded for a win; one point for a draw. Positions in the championship table are determined by points scored; where points scored are equal, positions depend upon goal average.

The final positions in the championship table are:

1, City. 2, Spurs. 3, Villa. 4, Arsenal. 5, United. 6, Rovers.

Four teams score the same number of points.

Ten goals in all are scored in the competition, three of these by the City. The Rovers, alone among the competitors, do not score a single goal.

The Villa beat the Spurs by 1 goal to 0.

The City beat the Rovers by 3 goals to 0.

Had the scores in this latter game been reversed, the Rovers would have won the championship.

What was the score in the game between the Arsenal and the United?

· 19 ·
SIX AUTHORS IN SEARCH OF A CHARACTER

Six authors are seated three a side in a first-class railway compartment. Their names are Black, Brown, Gray, Green, Pink and White. They are (but not respectively) an Essayist, an Historian, a Humorist, a Novelist, a Playwright and a Poet.

Each has written a book which some other occupant of the compartment is reading.

Mr Black is reading Essays. Mr Gray is reading a book by

the author sitting opposite to him. Mr Brown is sitting between the Essayist and the Humorist. Mr Pink is sitting next to the Playwright. The Essayist is facing the Historian. Mr Green is reading Plays. Mr Brown is the Novelist's brother-in-law. Mr Black, who is in a corner seat, has no interest in history. Mr Green is facing the Novelist. Mr Pink is reading a book by the Humorist. Mr White never reads Poetry.

Identify each of the six authors.

• 20 •

BETTY'S CIPHER

In the absence from duty of Miss Georgina Pawl, form-mistress of the Upper Fourth, Miss Auburn Head took her place. On the first day Miss Head intercepted the following message from Betty to one of her form-mates:

8MAP85M DAP85M DU33568 263 D5M B24 8AJ 2 EAS3 263 DP2D4 95SS 35M 9B5SM 4BM4 2921 BMP JB26HSM44 NA7 95SS 7M DMPGAPZM3 71 8568MP6A7.

Miss Head could not read it. *Can you?*

• 21 •

THE EARLY ENGLISH LEAGUE

Six teams take part in an Association Football competition: the Britons, the Saxons, the Normans, the Danes, the Angles and the Jutes. The competition lasts for five rounds, each team playing each of the others once. Two points are awarded for a win and one for a draw. Where points are equal, positions in the competition table depend on goal average, i.e. upon the ratio borne by the number of goals that a team has scored to the number of goals scored against it.

In the first round every team scores. Two teams each score two goals.

At the end of the first round the positions in the table are: (1) Britons, (2) Normans, (3) Danes, (4) Jutes, (5) Angles, (6) Saxons.

At the end of the second round the Normans have 4 points and the Danes have 2.

At the end of the third round the Angles have 3 points.

At the end of the fourth round the Jutes have 1 point.

At the end of the fifth round the Britons have 8 points and the Danes have 4 points.

Sixteen goals in all are scored in the competition.

Construct the final competition table, showing the number of matches won, drawn or lost by each team and goals scored for and against.

• 22 •

MR SOUTH

In a Contract Bridge match, the score is love-all in the second game. The players sitting East and West have won the first.

The player sitting North is the dealer.

Messrs North, South, East and West are taking part in the game. Only one of them occupies at the table the seat corresponding to his name; and this player takes no active part in the bidding.

The bidding is throughout reasonable. No player's bid, pass or double can fairly be regarded as unjustified.

Mr South plays the hand at three spades, doubled, and is defeated by 1400 points.

Mr West holds five spades to the queen.

Mr North's hand is as follows:

♠ 7 4, ♥ K Q 6, ♦ A K 7 5 3, ♣ K 3 2.

Where is Mr South sitting, and who is his partner?

• 22 •

OPEN-TOP BUSES

(Composed by Mr F. G. B. Atkinson)

"Why should I always travel by these stuffy covered-top buses?" thought Mr Brown. "I know there are a few open-top buses about and I'll keep count of them when I go to see Jones next Sunday."

The service concerned is Route 59, Camden Town and Coulsdon. The buses leave each end at 8 a.m. and then regularly every 10 minutes. The journey occupies 95 minutes and the buses wait 5 minutes at each end.

Mr Brown lives near Piccadilly Circus, 15 minutes from Camden Town; Mr Jones lives at South Croydon, 20 minutes from Coulsdon.

Mr Brown leaves Piccadilly Circus at 10.15 a.m., and alights at South Croydon at 11.15 a.m. Counting the first bus he passes (going towards Camden Town) as No. 1, he finds that Nos. 3 and 12 are open-top buses, the others being covered-top.

Returning from Mr Jones's house, Mr Brown leaves South Croydon at 7.50 p.m. and alights at Piccadilly Circus at 8.50 p.m. All the buses he passes (going towards Coulsdon) are covered-top except for one group of three open-top buses in succession.

How many open-top buses are there on the service, and what are their numbers in the series (reckoning No. 1 as mentioned above)?

• 24 •

THE PROFESSOR'S DAUGHTERS

The Professor was having breakfast with his daughters. "Listen", said Mary, "to the curious conditions drawn up by the Bazaar Committee:

'No article is to be priced at more than 5s.'

'Every article is to cost an exact number of shillings.'

'There are not to be more than two prices at any stall.'

'No two stalls are to have the same range of prices.'"

"How much will you give us to spend?" asked Martha.

The Professor made a rapid calculation.

"I will give you £4. 9s." he said. "You are to spend it all at one stall; no two of you will spend the same amount; and each of you will buy a present for me and a present for each of the others."

"Which stall are we to spend it at?" asked Mary.

The Professor laughed, "I am afraid you will have no option."

How many daughters has he?

• 25 •

NEWS FROM A SPY

Utterland and Depravia were at war. At an early stage in the proceedings Zymenoff, the notorious spy, was arrested by the Utterlanders at Eastport. He had on his person a copy of the following message:

"*Code* 10

TBTNR	OESAM	RLTDN	RRWNI	AEORI
TSIDD	NLDEN	EFLTN	SEADE	DOLOI
PAYII	FUPMG	OVENN	ORAOH	REIFC
USSRT	TSGAH	RUSRZ	IEHNG	DBSOY
NATTU	EMEWM	FSERN	SAAAE	LTEYS
TRLBN	EPNFE	RIIOO	XOHOS	ONSUF
IRUUC	YELTF".			

The Utterland Secret Service had little difficulty in disentangling Zymenoff's message. Can you?

• 25 •

COLONEL BLOTTO

Doubts having been expressed as to Colonel Blotto's competence, he was sent for by his General.

"Here", said the General, "is a little problem for you.

"There are four fortresses in the mountains. They are occupied by three hostile units, each under an independent command. The distribution of these units among the four fortresses is not known.

"You are in command of four units. You are to issue orders for the immediate occupation therewith of one or more of the mountain fortresses.

"Points will then be awarded on the following basis:

"If in any fortress you have more units than the enemy (or if you have one unit or more in a fortress not occupied by the enemy) you will count one point for possession of the fortress and one point, where the enemy is in occupation, for every unit in the outnumbered enemy force.

41

"If in any fortress you have fewer units than the enemy, points will be counted against you on exactly the same basis.

"If in any fortress you and the enemy have the same number of units, neither side scores as far as that fortress is concerned.

"A unit cannot be divided, either by you or by the enemy.

"Your object will be to issue such orders as will secure to you a maximum expectation of points."

What orders should Colonel Blotto give? And what are the odds, if he gives the right orders, against his actually losing points?

• 27 •

FAMILY BRIDGE

A family party, consisting of Mr and Mrs Smith, Mr and Mrs Brown, Mr and Mrs Jones, and Mr and Mrs Robinson (husband and wife in each case) make up two tables at bridge. Robinson plays with his daughter. Brown plays against his mother. Jones plays with his sister. Mrs Smith plays against her mother. Brown and his partner have the same mother. Smith plays with his mother-in-law. No player's uncle is participating.

Who partners whom, and how are the two tables made up?

• 28 •

RAIN

Extract from a letter from Jones:

"My brother and I have just been away for ten days' holiday. For both of us it started on the 1st and finished on the 10th. He went to Shrimpton and I to Prawnville.

"Before going we arranged with Sinkham, of Lloyds, for a policy of insurance against rain. Each of us was to receive £1 for a wet day following a fine one; £2 for a second consecutive wet day; £3 for a third consecutive wet day, and so on. Thus for five wet days alternated by fine ones, either of us would get £5; but for five consecutive wet days, £15.

"In return for these benefits, each of us would pay £1 per day for every fine day he had.

"These policies were a good investment. We both had it fine on the first day, and fine on the seventh; but we had fourteen wet days between us. My brother received from Sinkham £11 more than I did."

How much did Jones and his brother receive between them?

· 29 ·

THE MAD MILLIONAIRES

Two Chicago millionaires, Blosheim and Blum, are both anxious to get married. Neither, unfortunately, is physically attractive and their overtures are consistently rejected.

Eventually, however, Blosheim makes the following terms with six young ladies working for a film corporation at Hollywood:

For six nights running one of the six will meet Blosheim at an agreed rendezvous for dinner. He will not be told beforehand which of the six it is to be. Each night he will take with him a sealed envelope containing one of these ladies' names, and will deposit it on his companion's plate. If, when she opens the envelope, she finds her own name there, it is agreed that she will marry him.

There is nothing to debar any one of the young ladies from appearing more than once at the rendezvous.

Blum, impressed by the terms of this ingenious, and indeed thrilling, gamble, makes a somewhat similar arrangement. In his case, however, his choice is limited to five young ladies; he is only allowed three opportunities of writing down the correct name; and it is agreed that the same lady cannot meet him more than once.

Which of these two lunatics has the better chance of getting married, and what are the chances that two bachelors return to Chicago?

• 30 •

PUSCHOVSKI

It is certain that when Puschovski was arrested he had on his person an assignation with Korniloff, whom the police of three capitals were seeking. But all that could be found was a page torn from a note book:

"Angina	p. 169	Balmoral	p. 211
Antimony	p. 92	Barbary	p. 193
Apollyon	p. 38	Basilisk	p. 145
Apperception	p. 32	Bdellium	p. 96
Arianism	p. 15	Bedouins	p. 147
Aristarchs	p. 47	Betony	p. 50
Arthropoda	p. 98	Billiards	p. 203
Artillery	p. 128	Biscay	p. 155
Asphalt	p. 123	Blenheim	p. 147
Asphyxia	p. 252	Boswell	p. 94
Assizes	p. 37	Bow Street	p. 77
Asymptote	p. 94	Brazil	p. 80
Ataraxia	p. 184	Bridewell	p. 207
Autocracy	p. 30	Bromide,	see Bromine"

Where and at what time was Puschovski's assignation?

• 31 •

PLUTOCRATS AT PLAY

Two plutocrats, Goldstein and Swagg, met in friendly rivalry over 18 holes at golf.

They agreed to play for stakes on the following curious basis:

Stake money to be payable *after each hole* on the position of the game then obtaining.

A player one up at any hole to receive £1 from his opponent; a player two up to receive £3 (i.e. £1 + £2): a player three up to receive £6 (i.e. £1 + £2 + £3): and so on.

After five holes had been played, Goldstein owed Swagg £17.

After thirteen holes, neither player owed the other anything. Goldstein won the fourteenth and fifteenth.

The last three holes were halved, but at each of these Swagg missed a short putt through nervousness. They should all have been his holes.

What did these three missed putts cost him?

• 32 •

FUN ON THE 'PHLEGMATIC'

A, B, C, D and E are all enthusiastic solvers of conundrums. They are fellow-passengers on the S.S. *Phlegmatic*. They therefore agree to amuse themselves as follows:

(1) Each day one of them (the five taking it in turn) sets five conundrums for the other four to solve. The first to solve each conundrum scores one point. In no case can a point be divided; should two solvers claim to finish simultaneously, the point is awarded in accordance with the setter's decision. Five points, and no more, are awarded each day.

(2) At the end of each day each of the four solvers competing that day becomes entitled to £1 per point in respect of the difference in points between his score for the day and the score for the day of each lower-ranking competitor. The money owing from each solver who on balance has lost is paid each day into a pool from which those who on balance have won then draw their winnings.

The order of capacity, as solvers, of the five participants is: A, B, C, D, E. None of these is ever beaten, in respect of the number of conundrums solved in a single day, by a competitor ranking lower in order of capacity.

The sums paid into the pool on the first five days total £41 in all.

At the end of these five days A has won £20; D has lost £12; E has lost £12.

How much, on balance, has been won or lost by B and C respectively?

· 33 ·

CUBICLES

Professor Calculus gave each of his sons a large wooden cube. Each cube had each of its six faces painted a bright, cheerful colour.

Said the Professor to his sons:

"I want each of you to assign to each face of his cube one of the numbers 1 to 6. Then write this number in each corner of the face assigned to it.

"Next, take your fret-saws, and cut each cube into eight smaller ones. Each of these cubes will then have three numbered and three unnumbered faces. The sum of the numbers on its three numbered faces we will call its 'Total'."

The sons did as they were told, and in a short time each of them produced for inspection his eight smaller cubes (or "cubicles").

"Good", said Professor Calculus. He examined the cubicles. "I now set aside two of these; one has a Total of Nine and the other a Total of Seven. I put the remainder of the cubicles into a hat. If I draw one out at random the chances are two to one against its having a Total of Nine.

"How many cubicles in the hat have a Total of Fourteen?"
What is the answer?

· 34 ·

FOOTPRINTS IN THE SNOW

Old Miss Pennywise lived with her nephew, Richard, in a bungalow on Broccoli Heath. It is about 300 yards from the bungalow to the nearest highway.

On Boxing Day, 19—, Miss Pennywise had given both of her servants a holiday for the day, and their movements are satisfactorily accounted for.

Richard Pennywise left the bungalow at 10 a.m. to play golf. He is known to have been at the Broccoli Heath Golf Club (or on the links) from 10.30 a.m. till 5.40 p.m. At 4 p.m. it had begun to snow. He could not have reached the bungalow before just on 6 p.m. The snow ceased at 5.05 p.m.

At 6.05 p.m. a telephone call from the bungalow informed Chadbury Police Station that Miss Pennywise had been murdered. It was a man's voice. Inspector Guy at once set off. He reached the nearest point on the highway at 6.32 p.m.

He here discovered by the roadside the body of Richard Pennywise. He had been shot at close range through the head. A revolver lay at his right hand; two chambers had been discharged and Richard's were the only fingerprints to be found on it.

Richard had been dead for about ten minutes.

Inspector Guy proceeded to the bungalow. Here he found at 6.40 p.m. the body of Miss Pennywise, who had been shot through the heart. There was no trace of any weapon. She had been dead for at least an hour, but for less than an hour and a half.

Snow had fallen uniformly to a depth of about half an inch. Inspector Guy hastily searched the surrounding heath for footprints. None were to be found except those of Richard Pennywise, returning to the bungalow and proceeding thence to the point on the highway where his body was found. It is certain that Richard, and Richard only, was responsible for the footprints.

Close by were found the wheeltracks of a car, which had evidently been stationed at this point. These were afterwards proved to be the tracks of a car belonging to Richard's brother Vivian.

The police are satisfied that the murderer was one of the four beneficiaries under Miss Pennywise's will.

The police are right in thinking so.

The beneficiaries were:

(1) Richard Pennywise.

(2) Vivian Pennywise, his brother.

(3) Clara Poundfoolish, their cousin, engaged to Vivian Pennywise.

(4) Kitty Poundfoolish, her sister, at one time engaged to Richard.

Their respective movements are found to have been as follows:

(1) *Richard*—as stated above.

(2) *Vivian*. Lunched with Clara at her house in Chadbury. They then went to the local Picture-House where they are known to have arrived at 3 p.m. They state that they left the Picture-House at 4 p.m., but this is not corroborated. At 4.30 p.m. Vivian was seen by friends waiting for Clara outside her house. He told them they were going for a drive. He can prove that he was waiting continuously from 4.30 until 5.40 p.m. Clara's house is eight miles from Broccoli Heath. Vivian and Clara returned from their drive about 8 p.m.

(3) *Clara*—see above.

(4) Kitty. She states that she had arranged to lunch with Miss Pennywise, and that at 1.30 p.m. she found the old lady in excellent spirits. After lunch they walked round the garden. Kitty said Goodbye to Miss Pennywise in the garden just after 4 o'clock. Several witnesses saw Kitty depart, and can vouch that Miss Pennywise walked once or twice round the garden and then went indoors. Kitty reached a bridge club in Chadbury at 4.40 p.m. and can prove she was there until just on 6 p.m. She was called to the telephone at about 5.50, and was heard to say "I'll let him know at once, darling." She then left the Club.

Who murdered Miss Pennywise—and how?

• 35 •

CRACKRIB'S DIARY

Crackrib spent five years in Dartmoor for house-breaking. He bore an exemplary character, and devoted his spare time to study; his special interest being mathematics. He spent many months in copying out tables from a book of logarithms, and was permitted by the authorities to take these copies away.

Subsequently, Crackrib published a sensational "Diary" of Dartmoor life. The following is a specimen of the "firsthand material" on which his "Diary" was based:

Logs	Nos. 5050	5051	5052	5053
0	703 2920	703 3714	703 4665	703 5523
1	3015	3819	4718	5595
2	3084	3920	4805	5664
3	3151	4015	4920	5720
4	3225	4112	4988	5828
5	3310	4204	5065	5935
6	3421	4313	5125	6019
7	3497	4435	5219	6123
8	3567	4523	5320	6201
9	3639	4608	5415	6277

Can you decipher the entry?

(This cipher is based upon a episode which is stated to have actually occurred.)

• 36 •

TAKING A CHANCE

Three criminals, Arsen, Burgler, and Crooke, have decided to waylay and rob an old miser. It is agreed that one of them shall carry out the assault, while the other two keep watch. But which of the three shall it be?

After some discussion, the following novel plan is agreed upon. The key man is to be chosen by lot; each of the three conspirators having three votes, which he can distribute as he pleases among his confederates and himself. The robbery is to be carried out by the one who gets most votes.

All swear that there shall be no collusion in the voting.

It is further agreed—to encourage some measure of risk-taking—that the conspirator who gets most votes and the one who is next to him in the poll shall between them share the bulk of the swag.

Arsen like his colleagues is anxious to secure second place. Before voting, he makes the following calculations. The job is an unpleasant one and none of the three is anxious to carry it out. Burgler, who is timid, will most certainly not give any of his three votes to himself. Crooke, however, is more likely to take a chance; and Arsen is practically certain, from a remark which Crooke has made, that the latter (to improve his chances) will give himself one vote.

Given these assumptions, how should Arsen distribute his own three votes?

• 37 •

THE SECOND BLOTTO PROBLEM

Colonel Blotto having passed his first test, his General gave him a second.

"This time", said the General, "you are defending three mountain fortresses, which I will call A, B and C. You have four units wherewith to occupy one or more of them.

"A hostile force, of the same strength as yours (four units), is attacking these three forts. At the conclusion of the attack, points will be awarded on the following basis to you and to the opposing commander:

"For the possession of Fort A—4 points.
             "   "   B—3   "
             "   "   C—2   "

"For every enemy unit outnumbered in any of these fortresses—1 point.

"Where both sides have an equal number of units in a fortress, the points in respect of that fortress will be divided.

"The object, both of you and of the enemy commander,

is to secure, in making your dispositions, the maximum expectation of points.

"The enemy commander is informed, in the first instance, that he is to make his dispositions on the assumption that any one of your units is equally likely to be in any of the three forts. He is next told that you have been informed of his instructions, and are prepared to defeat such dispositions as he would naturally be making. He is not told that his knowledge of your acquaintance with his original instructions has been communicated to you.

"Dispose your four units so as to be certain of defeating the dispositions which your adversary will now make."

State and justify the Colonel's dispositions.

• 38 •
NEVERLAND

By way of consolation for some unkind criticisms in the press, General Givham-Biennes is made Military Governor of Neverland. The General has under his command one hundred military units.

There are three garrison towns in Neverland, which bear the somewhat unfortunate names of Day, Night and Morrow.

On July 1st, 19—, General Givham-Biennes' units are distributed among the three towns.

At 8 a.m. that day (08.00, military time) he broadcasts the following order:

"UNITS NOW AT DAY WILL PROCEED TO NIGHT TO MORROW STOP UNITS NOW AT MORROW WILL PROCEED TO DAY TO NIGHT STOP UNITS NOW AT NIGHT WILL PROCEED TO MORROW TO DAY".

At 6 p.m. (18.00) he broadcasts:

"ORDERS GIVEN THIS MORNING FOR UNITS TO PROCEED TO NIGHT ARE CANCELLED AS FAR AS UNITS WHICH HAVE NOT YET MOVED ARE CONCERNED".

And at midnight (23.59) he announces:

"UNITS WHICH WENT TO DAY TO NIGHT WILL RETURN AT DAYBREAK TO MORROW".

It may be taken that the General's idea of "day" (considered as a time-unit) is the period ending at 6 p.m. (18.00) and of "night" the period between 6 p.m. and midnight.

On July 3rd, the distribution of the General's forces were as follows:

At Day:	26 units.
At Night:	24 units.
At Morrow:	50 units.

Assuming that, where an order appears to be capable of two interpretations, half the unit commanders to whom it might apply interpret it in one sense and half in the other, what was the distribution of the General's forces at 8 a.m. on July 1st?

• 39 •

THE 'PHLEGMATIC'S' RETURN VOYAGE
(See *Fun on the 'Phlegmatic'*, p. 43)

On the *Phlegmatic*'s return voyage, six solvers, *A, B, C, D, E* and *F*, participated in the conundrum competitions. Each of the six in turn set daily six conundrums for the other five to solve. As before, one point was awarded by the setter to the solver of each conundrum. The order of capacity of the solvers was *A, B, C, D, E, F*; none of whom was ever beaten, in respect of the number of conundrums solved in a single day, by a lower-ranking competitor.

At the end of each day each of the five solvers competing that day became entitled to £1 per point in respect of the difference in points between his score for the day, and that of each other competitor. Settlement was effected daily by the payment into a pool, by each competitor who that day had on balance lost money, of the amount which on balance he had lost. The winners then drew from the pool what was due to them.

At the end of six days the amounts paid into the pool totalled £78. On no two days were the amounts paid in the same.

A had won £60 in the six days. *C* had lost the same amount each day.

How much on balance had been won or lost by B?

• 40 •

ALF'S LAST BID

The police were rounding up suspected members of Jack ("Mossyface") Clubb's murder-gang, in connection with a series of outrages, in particular the disappearance of "Gentleman" Jess. Jess is believed to have been made away with in Dublin.

Alf Aarons was "pulled in" at Fishguard. The following was found among his papers; for reasons which may (or may not) be apparent, it aroused the suspicions of the C.I.D.:

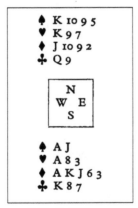

Underneath was scribbled: "There are 52 cards in the pack; this gives you a double chance. Both hands are a bit muddled."

What is the significance of these innocent looking "hands"?

CROSSWORDS

CROSSWORDS

1	2	3	4	5	6	7	8	9	10	11	12	13
14					15					16		
17	18				19				20			
21			22				23	24				
25				26			27			28		
29					30	31	32		33			
34		35					36					37
38			39			40		41	42		43	
44				45		46						
47					48		49					

SALOPIAN

(References in Italics)

ACROSS

1. *One of the quietest places under the sun.*   12. *See 35.*
14. My lore is not necessarily ancient.
15. *rev.* Rhizome or lace.
16. *When this and 25 dn., I got good advice from a wise man.*
17. Burning, and with wrath in it too.
19. Seek your employer in a tangled plot.
20. Shakespeare clad me in a russet mantle.
21. *rev.* Term applicable to maidenhood.
22. Average, or perhaps below it?
23. Doctor, thou lovest—on the stage.
25. *I and 10 dn. are ashes under 3 dn.*   27. *See 31.*
28. 16 and 25 *dn.* are of me.   29. *By me the broom blows.*
32. College near Lincoln.   34. He's just back again.
35. *With 12 ac., stone from the Isle of Portland.*
38. *Look for me on the graves of unlucky lovers.*
40. Presumed end of the Palladium.
42. Collapse of an upward flight—and on the river.

44. Thus are vulgarly described the offspring of mis-
cegenation.
46. *My flowers lie thick in field and lane.*
47. *rev.* Associated with a Lord Chancellor's namesake.
48. I was aboard the ark with 45 *dn.*
49. *My chimes play The Conquering Hero Comes.*

DOWN

1. *Blood is a rover, but I lie still.*
2. Indicates the spectacular.   3. *See* 25 *ac.*
4. *rev.* Colours often, but seldom those who carried them.
5. Harmonious joy.
6. Work is in this category: so are rheumatism and cold
mutton.
7. *rev.* A one-time officer loses his "gee".
8. *He keeps his house all kinds of weather.*
9. 15 *ac.*, is not.   10. *See* 25 *ac. and* 3.
11. Apparently William I looked forward to my day.
12. To torment in old French.
13. Gases are this that lie low.
18. The question is, what is behind it?
22. I'm not so obstinate if you walk in me.
24. *rev.* Caesar's wife, above suspicion.   25. *See* 16 *ac.*
26. Not an intelligence test but a measure of capacity.
27. Multiply with 45.
28. *rev.* Associated with an island in the Thames.
30. Alumni et alumnae.
31. *With* 23 *ac., Domesday is a long way further.*
33. Found in a bean, with the vitamins.
35. Citadel in ruins.
36. You might give £1 for this.
37. Much blown-about straw.
39. Familiar enough in Paris after 45 *rev.*
41. Austrian reverse reversed.
42. On the Turf, my plural has no singular.
43. Our's an inversion.
45. *See* 48 *ac.* and 27 and 39.

1	2	3	4	5	6		7	8	9	10	11	12
13						14	15					
16		17		18		19	20					
21						22		23			24	
25	26		27		28		29			30		
31						32			33			
34			35	36		37	38				39	
40						41				42		
43					44		45					
46						47						

SIXES AND SEVENS

ACROSS

1. The Ram and the Bull.
7. Without is a Queen.
13. A division has three brigades; I have usually three divisions.
14. Often to be found in a light mantle.
16. Here is your own.
20. Liater.
21. Reverse reverse, and reverse again.
22 *rev.* Dual continent.
25. Known also as a Last Ditcher.
29. Half dime, said the referee.
31. Apparently in 8.
32. Tailless fish.
34. May linger when knowledge comes.
38. Release.
40 *rev.* In 33, once one of the nuts.
41. Self-origination.
43. One does this in imagination.

45 *rev.* Hold fast.

46. Much confused Sisera comes down to breakfast.

47. Pours out anyhow.

DOWN

1. Dat is Paris, potted.

2. American's idea of lunch-time.

3, 44. The poet called me fair.

4. It isn't quite the same.

5, 37. So stand our soldiers.

6. Cobbler's end.

8. You can take your pill without us.

9. Upturned skeleton.

10. Just take cover.

11. Sift.

12. Lamp's poise disturbed (how creepy).

15. Wicked in 57 ways?

17. Du Maurier's producer.

18 *rev.* I figured in a parable.

19. Lote-bush.

23. Aren't we all?

24 *rev.* The devil without his church.

26. M.T.R. (!!)

27. Garment a little abbreviated.

28. Offered to the Maid of Athens.

30. Contrived a heavy cut in the dhole.

33. *See* 40.

35 *rev.* Beloved of mathematicians.

36. Not quite "one under the eight".

37. *See* 5.

39. Orderly arrangement, and without any duty too.

42. Not among the 39 articles.

44. *See* 3.

45. Plato's well.

1	2	3	4		5	6	7	8	9		10	11
12				13				14		15		
16					17				18			
19		20		21	22		23		24			
25					26			27	28	29		
	30						31		32			
33			34	35	36	37			38			
39			40			41	42	43		44	45	46
47									48			
49						50						

MY DEAR WATSON

ACROSS

1. Potent, though I jingle no more.
9. 26 assumes a wooden appearance.
12. Friendly but with a rocky interior.
14. Where one poor lion had no Christian.
16. Mr Gumbril's trousers.
18. Pronouncements of babes and sucklings.
19. Eve got her teeth into me.
21. Singular Mr Cinders.
23. Caesar's himself again.
24. Every gauntlet has a silver lining.
25. Where the bats come from.   26. *See 9 ac.*
28. Almost a heroine.
30. College that the "House" might have been.
32. What the frieze looked like in the mirror.
33. A very palpable — thruster.
37. My greatness is a thing of the past.
38. What the fog does.
39. How yesterday began.
40. League of notions.

41. Not quite the deuce.
44. What Alice became, she was too.
47. Confusion in an autocrat of the lower deck.
48. A list to port in the Rue de la Paix.
49. Cut the leaves, and reverse.
50. The city is apparently only a cart-track.

DOWN

1. Turns putrefaction to life.
2. Roger Bacon and Count Fosco were.
3. Life in Montparnasse.
4. Invert and grow thin.
5. Reverse your affectionate reference to Mr Lincoln.
6. Initials of a prominent figure in the counter-Reformation.
7. Ghost of 33 *ac.*
8. Our curate is quate this.
9. The less popular type of cave-man.
10. 47 *ac.* is an example.
11. A distant prospect in Greece.
13. Topsy-turvy play.
15. One of our "bright little contemporaries".
17. Wrestled for the body of Alkestis.
20. Some advice to a drunkard has just turned up.
22. Makes good progress in Norway.
27. One of the things that a Babbit likes to be.
29. Reverse 40 *ac.* and get an expression of dislike.
31. Found in 1 *ac.*
34. 5 split me upwards; his most famous predecessor could not be me.
35. Return of Mr Turpin from York.
36. Lancaster's was a coloured one.
42. Between the fish and the bull.
43. Spouse of the preceding.
44. D.V.8.
45. While enjoying 3, we have lost our tail.
46. The ghost of Hamlet's father found Hamlet to be this.

BELIEVE IT OR NOT

ACROSS

1. A certain Major-General's knowledge of this subject exceeded that of a novice in a nunnery.
8. Limps to begin with, and is pretty dismal anyway.
13. Might well describe the denture of any self-respecting heroine.
14. When my snows are melted, the Oxus overflows.
16. Spectacles well-suited to Napoleon during the hundred days.
19. Up-to-date form of government.
21. The "nose" have it!
23. A diffusion where is is not.
24. A famous Republican.
25. Manifestation of a roving optic.
26. With 40 *dn. rev.*, what Mr Brummel gave himself.
27. Every one is a trifle confused.
28. *rev.* Indisposition.
29. A connection that is almost lacking in breadth.
30. We can put them up with 41.
31. Darby returns to Joan!

34. This is what you would get if you were Edison.
35. Take king and saint to the mill.
36. A bit of a deer.
37. Same as 26.
38. The best place for me to make play with.
39. The way back from Philippi.
40. Signs and tokens.
43 *rev.* Presumably not ideally.
44. Nice job for a Dutch uncle.

DOWN

1. The study of such specimens as 27.
2. Adam or Eve.
3. A dove without a hat.
4. Allowance for weight.
5. In the beginning.
6. Relating to the earthquake, and overturned by it too; the plot of it has totally disappeared.
7. Abbreviated part of Rin-tin-tin.
8. I'm not exactly red-blooded, and one of my vowels has gone wrong.
9. Pep after 7.
10. A good day for the Race.
11. What swallows do in April.
12. Mr Pusey ends heretically.
15. 7 is an example.
17. Sounds gloomy but is indehiscent.
18. Major with seven stars.
20. Sweepstakes are.
22 *rev.* Might be used to "retain" a Cockney's permanent wave.
32. Almost almost dark.
33. Cut one's corn.
40. *See* 26.
41. *See* 30.
42. Look for me in New England.

PER ARDUA AD ASPIDISTRA

(The words required, where the clues are italicised, are just anagrams of one or more consecutive words)

ACROSS

1. Almost the gist of an early non-Christian.
7. Growth in industry.
11. Given to Charles to build up the individual.
13. State that was overlooked at T-time.
14. A gamble leads us lily-wards.
15. Desolate.
17 *rev.* Apotheosis of John Barleycorn.
18. "In Chancery."
19. Mixed drinks? Well, you see the point!
20. The poet outstrips the estuary.
22. The lad had a form of elephantiasis.
23. Release.
24. Position of Polonius, relative to the arras.
26. The Bourbons never did this.
28 *rev.* The soldier may take this with his discharge.
29. A sky-pilot's ministry.

30. Add a good Conservative, and round we go.
32. Clockwork—to the *n*th power.
33. Common enough in Germany.
34. We are not yet out of our depth.
36. We are all mixed up, at Covent Garden.
37. So many metal ends.
38. If what is hid were not hid, I should blossom.
39. They seem to have selected Korea.
40. Not a Pharisee, anyway!
41. Suggests the playboy of French monkey-land.

DOWN

1. *Thus I, a she-aunt, a special place must occupy.*
2. *What time does our bus sail, ask the children?*
3. False enough, but there's solid meat within.
4. A tree beloved of the Cockney steersman.
5. Makes but an annual appearance.
6 *rev.* Local, but none the less objectionable.
7. *Now let us prance, tune in on the radio.*
8. An accursed root.
9. Of additive import.
10. The poet lisped in my plural.
11. *That is inane, negus drunk from egg-cups.*
12. *These parts, I said, are to be ceded to the crown.*
16. Reflect—but begin with a tot.
19. The Assyrian is renowned for these.
21. An ex-enemy, hardly dressed for parade.
22. The "Derbies" are a little muddled.
25. We seem to have got "the bird".
27. Beheading the Bishop, we attain a symbol of purity.
28. The Goths did this to Rome.
31. What naughty fish did this?
35. Conjunction with a nautical flavour.
36. What Carnera might do to you.

SWELL-FOOT'S DAUGHTER

ACROSS

1. Southernness of aspect.
13. Related to Lord and Lady Aster.
14. Foreshadows a swing to the left.
15. Misappropriate.
17. My Alexandria was built by Antigonus.
18. Playwright's ape.
19. Fairy.
20. Duke who is always in the neighbourhood.
21. Addition.
25. Crossword solver's mood.
27. Throttle with a bend in it.
30. Almost a miss.
32. Letter and cord for the rhetorician.
33. Part of an instrument before long.
34. Cinderless lily.
36. On the hind legs, Admiral.
39. Title for Wilhelm II.
40. Unbeautified levels.

41. Rope at Burlington House.
45. Delusion that starts in the passage.

1, 2. Scoffing, and loving not the light.
3. Mutual.
4. Article of *virtu* somewhat battered.
5. Mine is a West-end theatre.
6. Leads in prayer.
7. Musical number.
8. Geotropic legume.
9. Swell-foot's daughter.
10. Rodent, tail foremost.
11. *See* 24.
12. Your last rising but one.
14. Battle Cruiser.
16. The Great Mel's trade.
22. Familiar article at the Louvre.
23. Globetrotters' spiritual home.
24, 11. Philosophy that sounds like a new sort of humbug.
26. Tragical? Nonsensical?
28. Comes after the "flowers that bloom in the spring".
29. The poet called me girlish.
31. Turned up tight.
37. Just reverse 22.
38. Military commissariat before the war.
41. Symbol of the indeterminate.
42, 43. *See* 9; what's gone is gone; the rest is just anyhow.
44. Pertains to daybreak with an article.

DERANGEMENT OF EPITAPHS
(*The clues italicised are anagrams*)

ACROSS

1.   Johnsonian activity.
12.   A sandboy's chief proclivity.
14.   Salt? or a backward glance of one?
16.   A shock? There's just the chance of one.
17.   From birth—as one might say—inclined.
19.   My friend's to Papal sway inclined.
22.   Yes, yes, a little mammal he.
26.   Who does? Why, all the family
27.   *The centre's my locality.*
28.   Postponement of finality.
34.   Villain becomes vociferous.
35.   Ex mouth—it's metalliferous.
36 *rev.*   A fiddler, famed of old, appears.
37.   Just think whence all the gold appears.
38.   Receptive—end's a case, I know.
41.   Initials of a place I know.
42.   He isn't too intelligible.
46.   A witness might be eligible.

68

DOWN

1.   The Prince of Whales and such as he.
2.   Touch wood? Dark, dark to touch is he.
3.   A flowing back's intended here.
4.   *Your milk, Monsieur, appended here.*
5.   *Some puss, and likewise part of him.*
6.   In bottle? but how smart of him.
7.   Our wooden walls are metal now.
8.   The Thespians are in fettle now.
9.   Inverted nap—the skin takes off.
10. Plane in an upward spin takes off.
11.   Compel them to produce it all.
13.   In Lancashire, no use at all.
15. Manhattan, Bronx, are known to me.
18. It looks extremely prone to me.
20. *In love with asininity.*
21. For—or against—the Trinity.
23 *rev.*   Grow, or from state to state to pass.
24.   I think some bishops wait to pass.
25 *rev.* Who nowhere mapped with clarity?
29. Suggests particularity.
30 *rev.* "—Greeks and their gifts" (the phrase we know).
31. Found in the fire most days, we know.
32.   *A touch, a feature—both, it seems.*
33 *rev.*   The dear old three-toed sloth, it seems.
39. High honour, to our knowledge, is.
40. Suggestive of ontologies.
43. State Sherman gained admission to.
44. Hat, hatless. (Preposition too.)
45.   Infinitive 'twill indicate.

Your prowess, friends, now vindicate.

LOWER CRUSTACEAN

ACROSS

1. Referring to the title of the piece.
15. We have it, so the motion must decease.
16. With colour coming back, a flower I'd be.
17 *rev.* The Council of Nicaea was rude to me.
18. Do (19) mix the form of public worship set.
20. One element of four. (21) 'Tis gold we get.
22. Plan (23) what a desk contains. (24) It oughter go.
27. A bird can lift a heavy weight, we know.
28. The hump-backed ox is sadly knocked about.
30. A town in Ecuador, but I'm without.
32. An authoress whose name recalls '15.
33. The gentlemen who "rook" us, bean by bean.
34. Riter—on whom 'twere wrong our wrath to wreak.
35. Some gadgets of the High Priest's we must seek.
36. A snake-like fish of what's within deprive.
37. Here's Mount Chagrin, (38) Capone, (39) a set of five.
41. In bulk. (42) Play, palindrome. (44) Do, follow me.

70

45.   Richard the First. (46) Was moved from see to see.
48.   Then let it stand. (49) Inclined. (50) Here's
        Mummy's lad.
51.   Initials these of good King George's dad.
52.   I start like nothing, but no enginear.
53.   Note—number three. (54) My needs will soon
        appear.

DOWN

1.   At Census-time, particulars I claim.
2.   In Paris, I suppose, this might be fame.
3.   One of a set of five; inverted, too.
4.   A willow, with its end lopped off, would do.
5, 47. Porthos, perhaps, or Aramis might be.
6.   In prison (says the lady) look for me.
7 *rev.*   The L.C.C. and Gaius here ally.
8.   Teetotal river. (9) Men who'll do, or die.
10.   Inconsequent. Its tail, you'll find, is not.
11.   Take air in company? The very spot.
12 *rev.* A concert-monger. (13) Einstein's faithful muse.
14.   Cabbage, (25) and fruit. (26) Old headless King
        we'll choose.
29 *rev.* Blue stone. (31) J. Keats discoursed of me with skill.
37.   Not pretty? If I plan, I'm muddled still.
40.   See, little Edward stands upon his crown.
43.   In me, you're in position—upside-down.

MUSICAL CHAIRS

When the strings of our fiddles are rosiny,
When our pipes are attuned to the ear,
Then the daughters of Zeus and Mnemosyne,
If we seek them, will surely appear.

[*Note: The names of these ladies are all to be found in the puzzle. One of them has met with a temporary reverse.*]

ACROSS

1. Suppose we begin with what's put at the end?
12. The colour of yellowish clay,
13. So be it. It's mean but it's muddled, my friend.
16. What Galahad sought the wrong way.
17. A wash and brush up?
19. and in France (yes, in France)
20 *rev.* Appease is what I seem to mean;
22, 28. So now to attack let the party advance.
23. Here one of the Housemen is seen.
24. I visit the schools, and they cheer when I go.
25. What every good shot needs to be.
29. Though "yes" be retracted, it doesn't mean "no".

31.   You'll find hidden metal in me.
33.   My job is to talk—at four hundred a year.
34.   But the Lords is where I'm to be found;
36.   To get back our losses (39) just turn round the beer—
40.   In "hicks" I am said to abound.
41.   Olympia "reverses" (of *Hoffmann* I speak).
44.   A martyr, perhaps, or a road.
48.   You'll meet me in Stepney
50.   —I'm coupled with Greek.
51.   And mine is a prophet's abode.

DOWN
 2.   Fight on, shadow cabinet!
 4.   get led astray—
 5.   Recover what seems to be gone.
 6.   I flow—so I'm told—into Chesapeake Bay.
 7.   We stand on our head, at Toulon.
 8.   Whatever is, is; and at Oxford is, now.
10.   I was English "as spoke" long ago.
14.   Exiguous I.
15.   Is she tidy, the cow?
18.   An overturned shelter, you know.
21.   Confused, Ananias? You'd best run to ground.
26.   Now established in W. 1.
27.   An article [compound] in Paris is found.
32.   Make us all more desirous of fun.
33.   I'm due for an orison; bring in the mat.
37.   A crash at St Paul's comes to view
38.   If phut should go phut 'twould be something like
        that.
42.   Mixed oof.   (43) What old soldiers don't do.
46.   My limb may be twisted—I'll batter you still;
47.   But this one's quite easy to see.
49.   How much was bequeathed in the guinea-pig's will?
50.   In the glow of the fire—look for me.

1	2	3	4		5	6	7	8		9	10	11
	12			13		14			15		16	
17		18	19				20	21				
22		23	24				25	26				27
28	29			30		31			32		33	
34					35					36		
	37			38		39			40		41	
42		43	44				45	46				
47		48	49				50	51				52
53				54					55			

FOR THE LITTLE ONES

ACROSS

1. How like it is—and yet so warm inside.
5. My plot and I are muddled; trust me still.
9 *rev.* Our common ancestry has been denied.
12. A Masefield play's within; I'm empty, shrill.
14. If Caesar of a dog should write, 'twere I.
16. In Robbie's brook, and of the Chaldees, too.
17. Robin without his air—the years slip by.
18. Call forth. (20) An Eastern table-land will do.
22. Riddle. (24) Behold a messenger—in drink.
26. Join, good round oath. (28) At Gare du Nord will be.
30. Go sneakingly about. (32) A spice, I think.
34. And when you take a count—why then, you're me.
35. Cotton? or celluloid? (36 *rev.*) I'm long, they say.
37. Diseased. (39) The ox can't keep a decent course.
41. A coin becomes a god, up Trondjem way.
42. Columbia. (43) There appears a hostile force.
45. Old me was once of rottenness the type.
47. Remember—'tis a sahib that I need.

74

49.	A boneback (that's contorted you, you snipe).
51.	Fattish. (53) Some birds of cassowary breed.
54.	The salt's—located 'neath the chimney-stack.
55.	What mind and body seek is coming back.

DOWN

1.	A twisted weapon finds itself in fruit.
2.	I measure land, clothe beasts—come seek me now.
3.	Frustum. (4) The heart am I of tuberous root.
5.	Ancestral home [perhaps] of Chu-Chin-Chow.
6.	We're Sundae's children—full of glace, they say.
7.	Then bring me milk—I've turned an old friend down.
8.	Two-thirds. (9) Get up, and face the other way.
10.	Sez puss. (11) A bow? or Sybil's favourite town?
13.	No, not a quadruped—a hardy breed.
15.	Your local chieftains summon you to prayer.
19.	If Vi and I should eat—there's all you need.
21.	Enough: Canadian leaf is crumpled there!
23.	So Cockneys spoke of Joris; wear away.
25.	The old beans have the young beans well in hand.
27.	Ywest is ywest—and we must bake to-day.
29.	Blot out. (31) Now mix thy strains, Thalia's band!
33.	This railroad leader paralyses me.
34.	Were needed here the pen of Foch himself.
35.	The bishop's headgear, squashed, send back (says he).
48, 36.	Our shelves will show you what is "on the shelf".
38.	This lane, that has a turning, leads to gold.
40.	This above all, to thine own self be me.
44.	Nose, noseless. (46) Sheepdog of a General's fold.
50.	Yes, signor. (52) No, not yet; six months 'twill be.

1	2	3				4	5	6	7	8	9	10	11
12		13	14	15					16				
17						18				19		20	
21				22		23			24				
25	26			27			28	29		30			
31					32	33				34			
35		36		37				38	39				
40	41	42			43		44						
45										46			

THE THIRTEEN NATIONS
(*The Thirteen Nations have disappeared*)

ACROSS

1.   you moke! you donkey! now I meet my end;
6.   your end? be this word used.
12. thus (13) worthy sailor (15) our amphibious friend
     is thoroughly confused.
16. make merry then (17) a muddled sailor, too!
18.   moves (20) nor without an O.
21. resentment (22) and volition (23) flowing through—
24.   me for the child, you know.
25. Victorian singer (27) all the pains of Hell
28.   and my poor thoughts are here.
31. dismay? (32) there's two (34) bring up the guns as well;
35.   Horatian strains appear.
37 *rev.* 'tis Sandy's girl.   (38) hero of many an act,
40.   complete with yo-heave-ho.
42. first this, then that (44) anger let loose, in fact—
45.   with cheery smile aglow.
46. one step across the Channel. *That's the lot.*
     Quite easy when you've got them—is it not?

DOWN

1.	appointment—or a making o'er perhaps
2.	and so on—plain to see.
3.	mine is a stannic home. (4 *rev.*) those furry chaps,
5 *rev.*	as good as good can be.
6.	addition's called for? no, the magic pole.
7.	a weeding out appears.
8.	distinguished artist (9) our assembly roll
10.	o'erlook, no Engineers!
11.	I mean the part of Cho-Cho-San to play—
14.	what rapture now for me.
15.	the foxglove—is not here (18) just flies away;
19.	in short, artillery.
26.	with pride all tangled (27) here's where all alight.
29.	he's blind and upside-down.
30.	a rum affair—a lily "painted" white;
31.	giving King George his crown.
32.	divide (33) but look—there's Alfred's colour gone.
36.	it's not yet said. (39) some height!
41.	same as the last (43) inside this nest. *Keep on*
	and soon 'twill all come right!

1		2	3	4	5	6	7	8	9	10	11	12
13	14	15								16		
17		18	19		20	21				22		
23		24			25			26	27		28	
29				30	31			32				
33							34					35
36		37		38			39				40	
	41				42		43	44				
45					46				47			

SETEBOSH

(1, 15, 32, 33 and 34 across, and 10, 14 and 20 down are to be found in the *dramatis personae* of *The Tempest*.)

ACROSS

8.   Inspiring, say, fear or respect.
13.   The hound's lost his head, I expect.
16.   An apple, a day—
          Well, it's not quite for aye.
17.   Now adorn we the Lord Mayor elect.
20.   Let's hope that I've got the right ring.
22.   Here's a chance for our brightest young thing.
23.   Now twice, from midday,
          We take nothing away.
24.   A bow that's contorted I bring.
25.   Here's labour unrest—over there.
26 *rev.* It's chili, high up in the air.
29.   I'll serve—if I can—
          For the oxygen fan.
31.   A dance? Why, I've fifty to spare.
36 *rev.* "I said: I will 'list for a"—this.
37.   And here I am 'listed, I wis.

38.   From his rock, I suppose,
         The holy man goes.
39.   Mr Niwdlab? There's something amiss.
41.   They *have* made a mess of my steed.
42.   Here flourishes graft, like a weed.
43.   Reverse we the hunt.
45.   Bring my "tee" to the front.
46.   Related.
47.   And pleasure's her meed.

DOWN

1.   Here courtesans' rule has no end.
2.   To Malachi my books extend.
3.   No, Sir, I must go.
4.   My tower you all know.
5.   Here's your finish unfinished, my friend.
6.   O yes, I am all for the Pope.
7.   Deprive you of courage and hope.
8.   Heigh-ho! on his head
         Stands a writer who's dead.
9.   For her chick poor Minerva must grope.
11.   A grape for Tiberius grew.
12.   These things they allow me to do.
18.   Take shelter from me.
19.   Tnerappa rieh—see?
21.   Here's the horse in Haig's latest *statoo*.
27.   I can promise you plenty of wear.
28.   My promont'ry isn't all there.
30.   The bonny black tree.
32.   A quart, please, for me.
35.   They've eclipsed the ellipse, I declare.
40 *rev.* This is what Joan of Arc was, at first.
44.   By Tirpitz with reason was cursed.

         So finish our clues;
         Let us hope they amuse
And that no honest solver's "reversed".

1	2		3		4	5	6		7	8	9	10
11		12		13	14			15				
16					17				18			
19				20		21				22	23	
24				25			26	27				
28		29	30		31			32	33			
34	35				36						37	
38			39			40				41	42	
43				44	45				46			
47												

BIGOTRY AND VIRTUE

ACROSS

1. The Exchequer is blamed for the decline of these activities.
11. The May Queen asked me to call her this.
14. From stereos produce an avenger.
16. The bishop enfolds the child of Kanga; his fate has never been solved.
17. This, which Shylock was, is best when golden.
18. You'll find at Glastonbury, the reverse of Fortuna's wheel.
19 *rev.* A famous University.
20. Chamber in which Professor Piccard ascended.
24. Transmit my reassembled ends.
25. I come back with a whole mind.
27. My annals were short and simple.
28. Doorkeeper who knew wat was wat.
31. An early adventurer begins with gas.
34. You'll cotton on.
36. Muscular attachment of X and a Professor.
37. Stratified mineral with 42.
38. The wrath of Athanasius.
39. It is usually this to swallow 27 *up*.

42. A place already referred to (*see also* 37).
43. The silver riddle—you concur?
45. Something of a jar for you.
46. Betake.
47. In 1960, Mr Lloyd George and Mr MacDonald may be this.

DOWN

1. Verse that is not poetry, yet verse that is not *vers libre*!
2. Street of guineas.
3. Marie or Norddeutscher?
4. Case unknown to case law.
5. Common enough in the Delectable Duchy.
6. A far from permanent wave.
7. Province of a distant Dominion.
8. Sweet and temper.
9. Bull's interior that indicates equality.
10. A King of the Trinobantes.
12. Colour of a "gee" and dolorous after one.
13. Ethelred deposed.
15. A certainty you'll see my points if you turn me upside-down.
21. What roses become in December.
22. 33 after broaching the second keg.
23. Co-opt your member, and get a winner; invert, and I'm injured and headless.
26. Chaliapine head downwards; the portents are much confused.
29. Take counsel; labour for hire after fifty.
30. "The wine of life is drawn, and the mere lees"
    Is in a poor way too.
32. Curiouser and curiouser.
33. Very ancient mariner.
35. Therefore—the blood is spilt.
37. Confused preparation for Easter.
40. Tin that is three parts humbug.
41. Reverse infirmity.
44. Just for example.

WHEN WE WERE VERY JUNG

(*Clues are italicised*)

ACROSS

1.	*Our job, when we were very Jung,*
12.	*Unwilling to let go,*
15.	Has oft, perchance with *pain*, been sung—
17.	As the *broad-minded* know.
19.	The *same* day (21) *of a Roman god*
22.	A *colour splashed* was claimed;
23.	The *ages* through (24) *who digs* (how odd!)
25.	Must *mend a lute that's* maimed.
28.	While *one who is in spirits versed,*
33.	With *samples* (36) *of a wine,*
38.	(Since *rest* (40) a *number* still put first)
43.	Off *well-hashed bird* may dine.
44, 41.	Then do not *render fruitless* now
45.	*What may in time return;*
48.	*A science* there is, as all allow,
	That teaches how things burn.

82

DOWN

[The clues *down* have been given in *positional* order (reading from left to right).]

1.	My *manuscript* is *written o'er* –
2.	The *Soviet chief* may prate:
34.	His *way* (3) is *still* too apt to bore
20.	The *joint* (39) *episcopate.*
4 *rev.*	*Peruvian prince, and tail-less too,*
21.	With *two* of clubs and all,
5.	Comes, *heart and mind awry,* to view
29.	To *measure* something *small.*
13.	A *breastplate* that *no donkey* knows
30.	*With us full fond* might be;
6.	With *help* (22 *rev.*) *erased*, the prospect grows
7.	*In France,* too *black* for me.
26.	*Mon fils* (42) *a plant* (8) and *gold* (18) *all clear*
35 *rev.*	My *promontory* grace:
14.	Though Caesar's *river* disappear,
31.	*His works* are still in place.
9.	Come, *dexterous* (27) *prince of ballet fame,*
46.	Since *Uncle Sam's without,*
10.	The *sprig* (32) *annoyance* brings, you claim,
47.	But *I* am *twice* as stout.
16.	Who *gibbets* then (37) his *fowl reversed*
	(And why should such be sung?)
11.	Must spare our *feelings.* Safety first,
	Since we are very Jung!

1	2			3	4	5	6	7	8		9	10
11		12	13							14		
15				16				17				
18				19			20			21		
22	23		24		25		26		27		28	
29				30					31	32	33	
34			35		36	37						
38		39		40			41	42			43	
44			45					46				
47												

MINISTERING ANGEL

There was a willow grew aslant a brook
  That in the glassy stream his hoar leaves showed,
And there she met her end, who earlier took
  These tokens to her sorrow-crowned abode:

Across: 2, 7, 24; *Down*: 1, 12, 39.

ACROSS

11.   He's half a loafer, and he's all a lout.
13.   To get them "all het up"—but what about?
15.   Confused the distance, mineral and tree.
16.   Little by little source of food can be.
17.   Gold, partly; mountain, partly; all by ear.
18.   We'll make no bones about it—bone, appear!
19.   A rare beginning, and a common end.
20.   Mixed up, our way Mahometwards we wend.
21.   A single foot contains twelve thousand me.
22.   The witless one without his vowels we see.
28.   How versatile—receives, returns, recruits.

29. Some hint of castigation 'mongst the roots.
30. Take from its frame—it's nearly time for bed.
31. Telegram? Try typography instead.
34. *Dulce est desipere*—one takes the tip.
36. Thousand of millions; stir, the thing's a snip.
38. Thus one escaped who from an airplane fell.
42. Of more than puss, of provender, I tell.
44. Now "with a difference" you can wear your rue.
45. Expression of a native comes to view.
46. Builder, but hardly for the distant years.
47. Behold Miss Dot; and Carrie, too, appears.

DOWN

2. Though wan in sound, it might be full of blood.
3. If Trinculo were this, he'd rank as dud.
4. What would the oculist seek first at Kew?
5. And what does he who works with acid do?
6. One makes entreaty; see, their eyes are black.
7. Rejected plays these qualities may lack.
8. Reverse a saxhorn; be contiguous still.
9. The holy man needs air. Then, climb your fill.
10. These lads in pocket one would gladly put.
13. *rev.* Begin by car; go all the way on foot.
14. Confuse a queen and then re-mobilise.
23. Here Mr Horn to walk the ceiling tries.
25. I know not sin—draw pole to distant pole.
26. My tally bring, and thus your thoughts control.
27. *rev.* The lady's drink is spilt; I'll put you right.
32. Symbol of power—comparative of might?
33. What Caesar's dog dug up and overturned.
35. Though wedded long, our partnership she spurned.
36. A good long pull, though hair it largely be.
37. *rev.* My master is a judge of high degree.
40. Once more the good old bishop must intrude.
41. Miss Robsart waves her heels, in care-free mood.
43. You might be right, if wrong you chance to do.
46. An office that Elizabethans knew.

THE MAY QUEEN

ACROSS

2.   If you're *waking* (7) call me *early*, call me early, (10)
     Mother (12) *dear*;

16.   My *grape-like* eyes—(17) unless I'm *wrong*—at
     visions new shall peer.

19.   *Through* me (*as Cicero says*), Mother, (20) there's *a
     tree that blooms* today,

23.   So I'm *almost—almost—at peace*, Mother, since I'm
     to be Queen of the May.

24.   There's an *empress* I could be, Mother, (26) but *I've
     found it* no great catch,

28.   As the *fruit of electrolysis* (29) brings forth the *urge to
     scratch*;

31.   And *half my senses* leave me (32) like *a rodent*
     drowned at play—

33 *rev.*   *O'erpower* (34) *Tom Cobley's wife*, Mother, but I'm
     to be Queen of the May.

35.   I was over on *Tuesday in Paris* (37) where *one of
     those great lakes lies*

38 *rev.*	And a *jar* (39) of the plant *Avena* was emptied before my eyes;
40.	'Twas *the end* of *Louis Seize*, Mother, (41) as the *sexton* knows full well—
44.	My *age may not be known*, Mother, (45) but there's *college* lads could tell!
47 *rev.*	And *seated* there *at the Tuileries*, (48) 'neath the *headless prophet's* sway,
49.	I *mingled* my *tears* with theirs, Mother, for I'm to be Queen of the May.

DOWN

1.	There's *many a dark* dark face, Mother, (2) no *underlord* denies;
3.	*Likewise* (4) *a King* has marvelled at the darkness of their eyes;
5.	*Pounds* (6) from *a Grand Inquisitor* (7) this *version* might delay—
8.	That *each does a short-arm balance*, since I'm to be Queen of the May.
9.	*Encouraging* their *words*, Mother, (11) *where still Romance is kind*,
13.	But beyond the *fiery mountain* (14) *th' repellent ore* they'll find.
15.	'Tis there *the notorious sands* are—(18) they must *go some other way*;
19.	*Minstrels, the jetty's ruined*—but I'm to be Queen of the May.
21.	*Up, then* (22) and let's *with Ion* make *inroad*—sound the Horn!
25.	*Games* (27) for *the Beak*—(30) *he's muddled the Bicester with the Quorn*.
36.	*Turn up the second letter*, Mother; (42, 43) give *affectation* sway –
46.	*Inside of noon* they'll crown me, for I'm to be Queen of the May.

1	2	3	4	5	6	7	8	9	10	11	12	13
	14				15							
16											17	
18			19						20			
21		22	23	24					25	26		27
28				29		30	31	32		33		
34	35		36		37		38				39	
40		41				42		43				
44			45	46								
47									48			

VANITY FAIR

"Come, children, let us put away the box and the puppets."
Put them in 1, 16, 21, 34 and 44 across.

ACROSS

14. An old Spanish ocean am I.
15. "Nosey Parker" might well be the cry.
18. Indication of time I supply.

19. Here's somebody's calling for me.
20. A course, that is crooked, at sea.
28. Now reddened your litmus shall be.

29. My plural was sung with the man.
31. I'm of somewhat indefinite pan.
33. With my offspring, to pray you may plan.

40. For Kipling's harumfrodite seek.
41. Our me-shotten coast is unique.
42. Who invented the Bull-doggy clique?

43. Here's a boxer knocked clean off his nut.
47. Without us, your beer would go phut.

48. Reverse, and I'll but you a but.

DOWN

1. Ben Jonson, as everyone knows.
2. Uncle Jonath: that's clear, I suppose?
3. When gyring, 'tis thither one goes.

4. This Horace besought us to seize.
5. Thus sting (so says rumour) the bees.
6. A cocktail that's certain to please.

7. Some assertion—a shellfish and I.
8. Little darling will flower, by and by.
9. Add finely, and Venus you'll spy.

10. A pronoun, with gibus inside.
11. Mr Shelley his birdhood denied.
12. An em now be pleased to divide.

13. A shock for the citizens, this.
17. What birds do—symbolic of bliss.
21. Where Austria once faced the abyss.

22. Just a name; 27 well stirred.
23. This is March 25—so I've heard.
24. To admire him were doubtless absurd.

25. "Roll by"; there is shelter for you.
26. A cabin; disorderly, too.
27. Looks black—but it's pleasant to view.

30. With 42, "signals" regret.
32. The same one can easily get.
35. The Janeites say: very well met.

36. Mr Rat, they've extracted your tooth.
37. Take over—that's easy, forsooth!
38. Young in spirit, if seldom a youth.

39. A byword for courage was I.
45. ⎫ Disentangle four letters, and try
46. ⎭ A roll, or a stripe, to supply.

PRINCE OF DENMARK
(*The references to the play are italicised*)

ACROSS

1. Monmouth's password.
5. How sad if the bar were this up.
9. *We may call it herb-grace o' Sundays.*
12. *Hamlet's father had a station like Mercury, new-lighted on this sort of hill.*
15. Traditionally long.
16. Is Mr Huxley with us.
17. Early work of Dame Ethel Smythe.
19. And in Latin gives, say, Catullus.
20. Disorder in a famous battlefield.
22. Inner, that is without.
23. There's a sliced-up fruit in Alabama.
26. Plot with me.
27. Once famous as a prima donna.
28. Just leave this where it is.
29. The Premier puts the chart back.
30. Accident on the rink.
33. You had better get this colour on (!)

90

34. We seem to have attained unity.
36. *Raison d'être* of a fourteenth-century Bisley.
38 *rev.* An allowance of my plural was once thought proper for young men.
40. The pessimists say my kind is on the increase.
42. One of John Bull's other islands.
43. Voltaire's headless neighbour.
45. I can go off pretty quickly with 44.
46. You'll find me at the West end of Oxford Street.
47 *rev.* Here you have caught some Tartans.
48. *The satirical slave says old men's eyes purge this.*

DOWN

1. My rock proved five times vulnerable.
2. I suppose the poet's over.
3. *Laertes complained that this was not provided for his father.*
4. The egg of Columbus was this.
5 *rev. The rugged Pyrrhus became total this.*
6, 7. *By these, said Polonius, we find directions out.*
9, 8. Mr Hemingway's sun also this.
10, 44. *Hamlet's woe, as characterised by the King.*
11. Among the more popular complexes.
13. A king in Hanover.
14. My pose is hypothetical.
18. *The path of dalliance.*
21. Might help you with your income-tax return.
24 *rev.* You can get shrewd by dismantling a monument.
25. Gobbled infatuation.
26. *Hamlet applied this term to Rosencrantz.*
28. You can't, always.
31. Table-land after 29 *ac.*
32. *Wharf where the fat weed rots itself.*
35 *rev.* Americans get this in the neck.
36. Bone upside down.
37. The "poor little girl" is a bit confused.
39. Not often from the fruit of the fir-tree.
41. Topsy applied this term to municipal councillors.
42. Glimpse of Sir Hamilton's inside.

1	2	3	4	5	6	7	8	9	10	11	12	
13			14	15			16	17			18	19
20		21	22			23	24			25	26	
	27	28			29	30			31	32		
33	34			35	36			37	38			
39			40	41			42	43			44	45
46		47	48			49	50			51	52	
	53	54			55	56			57	58		
59	60			61	62			63	64			
65			66				67				68	

SPLITS

ACROSS

1, 14. Slow sort of test *you* do.

5, 13 *dn.* Trinculo expects you to do this.

9. The best-known one worked in an arboreal setting.

13. It's a little confused.　　　　　　　14. *See* 1.

16, 23. Alleged instrument of martyrdom.

18. The guts of Tin Lizzie.

20. Not alas, as not there.

21. Enough of them would take you round the circle.

23. *See* 16.

25. More powerful than the King.

27. Behead an exhibition of equestrian skill.

29 *rev.* Something for the consumer.

31, 24 *dn.* What Mr Wilde left to posterity.

33. Found inside corn.

35. Something astronomers never see.

37 *rev.* Sometimes it's a dry one.

39. A good beginning for a Scotsman.　　　40. *See* 28 *dn.*

42 *rev.* Themes without ease.

44 *rev.*, 46. How Mrs Gamp liked her gin.

47. A well-assorted get-up.

92

49. Here originated a philosophy.
51. Shakespeare said of this there was muoch.
53. You'll find my lode in the Thames valley.
55. Starts a show on the halls.
57. *See* 10 *dn.*   59. From Perusalem.
61, 48 *dn.* Where to look for Dominion.
63 *rev.* The beginning of a fairy story.
65. Internationally recognised.
66, 17 *dn.* Suggests a series of gallant failures.
67. *See* 39 *dn.*   68. *See* 12 *dn.*

DOWN
  2. Capital!   3. A current rises.
  4. Key up with 44 *rev.*
  6. Heart of the Hardy country.
  7. Belonging to a Roman god.
  8. A toupée in search of a head.
10, 57 *ac.* Of the earth earthy.
11 *rev.* My pose is Falstaffian.
12, 68 *ac.* Kipps liked it "buttud".   13. *See* 5 *ac.*
15. Not approved of by Mr Stalin.   17. *See* 66 *ac.*
19, 26. Bradshaw was a prominent one.
22. Can come down in sheets.   24. *See* 31 *ac.*
26. *See* 19.   28, 40 *ac.* Greatly deplete.
32, 30. Henry VIII knew them not.   34. *See* 43.
36 *rev.* The King's is obsolete.
38. My lady of the little black bag.
39, 67 *ac.* Describes the usages of words that Trinculo likes.
41. My banks are in Italy.
43, 34. One is advised to do this with transports.
45. Habitat of 52 *rev.*   48. *See* 61 *ac.*
50. Lord Astor is at home here.
52 *rev.* The doctors' dilemma.
54. The bravest of the brave.
56. The distorted soul of a Proust.
58. Look and you can't miss it.
60, 62. Part of a Province.
64. It's evident I've no ear.

BIOGRAPHY AND BOTANY

ACROSS

1. His ultimate fate resembled his grandmother's.
13. Planeless plane.
14. There seems to have been a wind on the heath, brother.
15 *rev.* Colleague of Mr Burke.
16. Gags that are useless to the gagged.
17. Shake up what was left in your glass to get the material for a stew.
18 *rev.* A few commissions pending.
19. Member of 13 *ac.* club.
20. Twisted weapon; twisted quarry.
21 *rev.* Not the kitchen range.
22. Edna found home to be this.
23. The White Knight's world.
24 *rev.* Thin sort of town.
25. Afterwards you can stir your tea between your hands.
27. Has neither end nor beginning.
29. Proclivities of Mr Trotter.
33. Just the place for an aunt.

35. Take back your assent, Monsieur, the obligation is muddled.

36. From and in China.

38. Conclusive enough with water.

39. Member of the Fringe family.

41 *rev.* They say the army moves on its stomach.

42. Gantry that supported very little.

43. Pontificated, but not at the Vatican.

DOWN

1. Long champion, and a challenger still.

2. Up-lift with a welcome ending.

3. Shocking taste in Philistia.

4. Tories or no Tories, the world still does this.

5. Kcud.

6. I seem to be all wrong.

7. 21 *ac.* in Spain.

8. There are quite a lot of these in the Pantomime.

9 *rev.* He'll be a big bird presently.

10. Scraps of a circumference.

11. Mr Mole's name for a friend of his.

12. Carried on without opiates; his great work is hidden there.

15 *rev.* Practise unkindness.

23. A wayside plant seems appropriately named.

24. Don Alfonso hasn't got one.

26. Gave a very successful imitation of a harpy.

28 *rev.* Pawns in the game of life.

30. Another of Mr Mole's friends.

31. Oh! to be in Paris—

32. Grimace, and an upward stagger.

34. *See* 40.

37. Mr Keats felt an inward moan to sit upon it.

40, 34. Obsolete court.

TWO BY TWO

Specific clues are not given for 2, 11, 13, 18, 25, 32, 43 and 49
rev. across, or for 1, 12, 14 *rev.*, 26, 31, and 35 down. In these
fourteen spaces are to be arranged the following pairs:

> The *genii loci* of a West-end rendezvous.
> Fore-runners of the Heptarchy.
> Two gentlemen easily "rattled".
> Oyster fans.
> Stars which commemorate an affinity.
> Navigators of a pea-green boat.
> *Sine quibus non* of the cocktail bar.

ACROSS

7. He is enshrined in every child's pantheon.
15 *rev.* Lover off his nut.
16. The Middle West's idea of Cleopatra.
17. Sounds a very odd lake.
20 *rev.* Evidently we can't skate.
23. Shelley says chameleons feed on it.
24. Pea's wings.

26 *rev.* Illustrious illustrator.

28. Was sickly after 41.

29 *rev.* One of the best-hated men in history.

30 *rev. See* 40.

33. Flies with a mingled tear following.

35. Gang your ain.

36. Pull the ears.

38. You want an "open" mind.

40. Not always welcome after 30 *rev.*

41. *See* 28.

42. Compounded of three.

44. Beginnings of black magic.

46. Knotted halter.

47. The reverse of tranquil.

48. One good bird deserves another.

DOWN

2. A pretty dry one.

3. Liquid mixed in solid.

4, 5. Wolf that suckled Romulus.

6 *rev.* What gents wear in Brooklyn.

7. Can't be danced without any.

8. Mother of James I and VI in trouble.

9 *rev.* I leave you, image.

10. Quite absorbing.

11. Team-mate of Mr Tittle.

19. You can be sure of one shell.

21 *rev.* Look for me on a sixpence.

22 *rev.* I act—in the past.

23 *rev.* One of the Craig family

24. Wheels within wheels.

27 *rev.* I had a certain Oriental charm.

34. Some more of the Middle West.

37. Distributed burden.

39. Nothing is lost in a foreign capital.

45. Half of 38.

ET EGO IN ARCADIA

ACROSS

1. Churchmen on both sides of the Atlantic.
14. One touch of this will make the world seem thin.
15. Accompanies little Constance at the concert.
16. Seat of the pard-like fever.
18. Bugbear of the late Oom Paul.
21. Habitat of Messrs Tin and Copper.
22. Love me love my stamp.
23. The man that film-fans love.
24. Perhaps this is above you.
26. A rare eagle's nest.
28. Master of Turkish delights.
30. Look on the reverse side too.
31. My purpose? Neck or nothing.
33. A liar has been deprived of a certain article.
34. Bread is the staff of life; and my life was described as "one long loaf".
35. What blackened Mr Micawber's outlook.
38. Sixteen a side.

40. Most of great-grandmother's petticoat.
41. Relates to optic distortion.

DOWN

1. Tree that breeds jujubes.
2. The spirit can move me.
3. Mirth.
4. See the waters boil up.
5. As it might be, Marconi.
6. Pretender curtailed and overturned.
7. Opens things up a bit.
8, 9. Mixture of brine.
10. Cicero's there.
11. Flo's flow.
12. The texture comes up.
13. They say that "business English" is often this.
17. Just lucre.
19. What Tweedledum and Tweedledee were fated to do.
20. Nix in Calais harbour.
25. Upheaval at the *White Horse*.
27. Remain in suspension.
29. I sound like a newspaper for illiterates; but turn me up and you'll find a classic.
31. Herdless herd.
32. Embers after a century; you can let the credit go.
33. Confuse the hunger of a Proust.
35. Distinction in the home of lost causes.
36. An Irishman's escaped from a bowl.
37. Dwelling, bed, or boat.
39. Part of 3.

AGAIN THE RINGER

ACROSS

1. Hesiod's first woman.
6. Exercise at Oxford or Cambridge.
10. Looking forward backwards.
16. Wave that baffled Knut.
17. Fruit after an interdict.
18. I was here and there in Tennyson and so was my friend
    the grayling.
19. This, dear reader, is an accurate description of you.
21. Boiled in bed.
22. Why not asseverate?
23. Turn again back.
24. There in Scotland goes the battered philosopher.
26. Care needs another five hundred; fifty would have
    served Achilles.
27. You can almost smell the river.
29. Little tin symbol.
30. Put an end to Clytaemnestra.
33. Toss the ball back.

35. Here you are returning.
37. Sounds like refreshments, but it's jewels.
40. Henry V sowed wild ones.
41. Well known in the Smith family.
42. Adventures in a laboratory.
43. Reverse what comes 'twixt magpie and bull.
44. One of the Prince's objectives.

DOWN

1. They asked Malvolio his opinion concerning wildfowl.
2. Not unknown to Trinculo.
3. Not a big knot.
4. A muddled fire-worshipper.
5. A Cockney is not.
7. West-end success.
8. Put in upside-down.
9. Harvest home on the Tiber.
11. Better sow 40 *ac.*
12. Vesta, get you down.
13. Sounds like a palmist's city.
14. Believe and the plant turned up.
15. Old awls that led to Aux.
20. Roderigo Diaz.
23. Inverted frame faces eastward.
25. Scene of Nero's command performance.
28. Muddy waters well stirred.
31. Fifty short of what is lawful.
32. Commercial transaction in Cheshire.
33. Reverse the stuff to give Hollywood.
34. "Eight good men in the good old times."
36. I have run out of rain.
38. The beginnings of hydrophobia.
39. And a prune's companion cut short.

WORD PUZZLES

WORD PUZZLES

These puzzles—unlike those which involve a knowledge of Mathematics, or a specialised interest in a game such as Bridge or Chess—require no technical equipment. There is no reason therefore why readers to whom they are new should not at once set about solving them. A short explanation follows of the various types of puzzle presented.

DOUBLE ACROSTICS

A Double Acrostic is really a crossword without its frame-work, and with only two clues "down". The problem is to find a series of words, to which more or less far-fetched clues are given, of which the first and last letters spell out two words more. These two latter words are the "uprights"; the others are the "lights".

Traditionally, an Acrostic is set out in verse and composers take pride in a presentation which is aesthetically satisfactory. It is legitimate to "reverse" a light (see below), or to leave out a part of a light, if indication that this has been done is given in the clues. A simple example follows:

UPRIGHTS

If at first you don't succeed
Here's the counsel that you need.

LIGHTS

1. *A broom—a monarch's emblem too.*
2. *This fellow won't take thought for you.*
3. *See, what's just alive returns.*
4. *Small article the monkey spurns.*
5. *Though with four of me you're blest*
   A mariner I'll still suggest.

105

The answer is

G E N I S T A
UNTHINKING
E V I L A
S   I   M   I   AN
S E A S O N

This illustrates the various tricks of the trade. Light 3 is reversed ("what's just alive returns"); light 4 goes without its "small article"; light 5 has a second meaning (sea-son).

ACROSTAGRAMS

(Invented by the writer) are just Double Acrostics of which the uprights are anagrams of one another (i.e. composed of the same letters). E.g.

INTERIM
T A V I –STOCK
E D I C T
M I C E

The reader might like to try his hand at constructing clues for this example.

The remaining puzzles are very simple.

ANAGRAMS

Are merely words of which the letters are jumbled up; ANTELOPE might become PANTOLEE or LEAN POET.

Where the letters of *two* words are jumbled, one gets a

DUOGRAM

Thus LION and TIGER give us LOITERING or TIE NO GIRL.

TWO POINTS OF VIEW

Presents clues to two words, of which one is the other one spelt backwards (RATS and STAR for example). Finally, a

DECAPITATION

Invites the solver to find a word which can lose its first letter to make another word, and can then lose its first letter again.

E.g. S T O U T
T O U T
O U T

There remain a few.

PALINDROMIC WORD-SQUARES

discussed on p. 126.

DOUBLE ACROSTICS

• 1 •

UPRIGHTS

To this one, nothing comes amiss,
While *that* admires the skill of *this*.

LIGHTS

1. Can be distinguished from a bird
     When the wind's set fair.
2. A "wild and woolly" state, I've heard,
     Though I've not been there.
3. "And where's your wife?" they asked. Said he:
     "Did you pass the salt?"
4. His witless greed has come to be
     A common fault.
5. A muse. Whoe'er obeys her laws
     "A-muses" still.
6. By some regarded as the cause
     Of every ill.

• 2 •

UPRIGHTS

You may "pick me up" (not a good thing to do),
And the harder I'm driven, the better for you.

LIGHTS

1. My street after Milton's more recently named,
2. That I'm last of my line has been often proclaimed.
3. On the bottle the Cockney sees what mayn't be true.
4. This episode, Eve dear, spelt trouble for you.

• 3 •

UPRIGHTS

Brother and sister. She was drowned, and he
Was slain in combat—inadvertently.

LIGHTS

1. Of doubtful morals, though in manner gay.
2. A "shocking" scientist—name cut half away.
3. I'm out of reach, yet every one is me.
4. Object of much contention (ask L.C.!)
5. This tangled story's valued in the East.
6. In Scripture, find the name of holy priest.
7. The surf beats loudly on this lovely shore;
   How far away? Say playfully, some more!

• 4 •

UPRIGHTS

The Name and Title of an English king.

LIGHTS

1. "Oo follows me"—a harbinger of spring?
2. What Henry, when in Paris, might become.
3. More than a song!—a heretic, to some.
4. Out out! But half the savoury mess remains.
5. Her charms provoked a poet's languorous strains.
6. One twists one's self about, to find an age.
7. Words, rearranged, in battle might engage.
8. This may be wit; but wisdom—that I doubt!
9. A crew's objective smartly turns about.
10. What would a stammerer do without his saint?
11. He sings, perhaps; or plays; or tries to paint.
12. 'Fore such as these, the unanointed bow.
13. He sold us proverbs. No-one wants them now.

• 5 •

UPRIGHTS

Oh, Mr Einstein,
   Surely you'd agree
That not so very long ago
   Great men were we?
But oh, Mr Einstein,
   Since to fame you've jumped,
Your stock's gone soaring up,
   And our stock's slumped!

LIGHTS

1. See the great hulking brute,
   Shorn of his tail.
2. In far Hawaii hear
   My music's wail.
3. Was the moon new or full
   When I went o'er?
4. No 'scaping from my lot
   (Pride of the corps!)
5. Do you like novel tongues—
   Answer I seek!
6. Here, I suppose, we'll find
   Stout Cortez' peak.

• 6 •

UPRIGHTS

I said, The outlook's none too bad,
And yet two suits were all I had.

LIGHTS

1. A "veg." is here (don't gammon me).
2. Behold the flattest sort of tree.
3. With this, one's mind is scarce at rest.
4. What cocktail suits the patient best?
5. The bright young things pronounce her slow.
6. Yes, some are Boojums—that we know.

111

• 7 •

UPRIGHTS

No doubt their history's largely lost,
 But this at least we know:
By them the flag was double-crossed,
 Two centuries ago.

LIGHTS

1. So logical, I've often heard.
2. Traditionally pert.
3. We introduce a tail-less bird.
4. An element inert.
5. I'm wrong—or so the lawyers say.
6. Here Sherman flouted Lee.
7. Utopia—spelt a different way.
8. A forest home for me!
9. I keep your "trunks" in good repair.
10. My neck provokes a grin.
11. A king, although we've room to spare,
  Has somehow not got in.

• 8 •

UPRIGHTS

An optimist (of sorts) is one,
 A pessimist the other;
And both, we're told, enjoy the fun
 Of "downing" one another.

LIGHTS

1. Though socially I'd prove a "flop"
  I've sometimes gone off nicely.
2. The widespread service of the "Shop"
  Is here summed up precisely.
3. A nineteenth-century "heroine" she
  (A child of glorious Devon's).
4. What sort of rainbow could one see
  Set in the starry heavens?

• 9 •

UPRIGHTS

And one of these, perchance, will suit
Before they clear and bring the fruit.

LIGHTS

1. We'll "take the count"—a strenuous start.
2. He took his dad's advice to heart.
3. Interior of a huge machine.
4. A sort of Parliament is seen.
5. The session tends to make us thin.
6. "Salt of the choir"? Yes, look within!
7. Full many a one our minds recall;
   Brutus the noblest of them all.

• 10 •

UPRIGHTS

My world was young, and, I suppose,
"Lasses were queens" and these were those.

LIGHTS

1. How apt the grumble that was heard
   When someone "tailed" the wretched bird.
2. Fitzgerald's Omar (how precise!)
   So qualified his paradise.
3. Archimedes, one calls to mind,
   Thus advertised his latest find.
4. He gave them wisdom, hot and strong,
   So long ago? Not *quite* so long.
5. Like Browning (R.), one still reveres
   The playwright's "dropping of warm tears".

113

• 11 •

UPRIGHTS

He showed his nice cravat to Alice—
A little present from the Palace.

LIGHTS

1. A tough guy this, whose whimsicality
   Found scope in infantile mortality.
2. A language; in the orient seek it,
   For that, I'm told, is where they speak it.
3. An easy clue. The veriest dullard
   Knows what by nicotine is coloured.
4. Here—such at least is my impression—
   The parish council meets in session.
5. Hither—and not to the Bahamas—
   I'd hie if I were hunting lamas.
6. Perhaps with joy, perhaps with sorrow,
   One calls to mind: 'twas once to-morrow.

• 12 •

UPRIGHTS

He "twanged the lyre" (yes, that's the right expression)—
   He twanged it with a will;
So furnishing the capped-and-gowned profession
   With sounds that echo still".

LIGHTS

1. "I will be good"—mark well her aspiration,
   (So'd we, if we knew how).
2. Land out of sight! The wrath of a harassed nation
   Is all that's left us now.
3. He modelled. And, if pickle follows after,
   A scourge for all 'twill be.

4. His black beard shook beneath Homeric laughter;
   His like we shall not see.
5. Their "warrior queen" well earned the poet's pity,
   In days now past and gone.
6. It ought to be, no doubt, a mighty city;
   Yet it has not got on.

• 13 •

UPRIGHTS

Here's My Lord; here, Sir, are you.
Of each, to start with, give me two.

LIGHTS

1. He wears his "lorals" on the Bench.
2. A "British King" begat the wench.
3. A tasty melange now display.
4. The novelist has lost his way.
5. One chapter's all that I can show.
6. One script on top and one below.

• 14 •

UPRIGHTS

"Who leads at the Bridge is unlikely to lose."
To think of the river just gives one the blues.

LIGHTS

1. Such are humming, and buzzing, and things of that kind.
2. At a pinch—here's a half-disarrangement to find.
3. Mussolini's invention; much vaunted, much cursed.
4. O a bluff, if confused; and he enters head first.
5. He might be from Blackburn; he might be a scout.
6. An old work of fiction, the wrong way about.
7. Lord Melchett the first? Or just one of the nuts?
8. This is all I had left after "cent per cent cuts".
9. A gay dog this "merchant of Venice", I guess,
   Was he more than a dog, though? The answer is—yes.

• 15 •

UPRIGHTS

Here the "old salts" are (be wary!)
   And *there* Mr Belloc roams free;
But put them together, and airy
   The hopes that are wafted to me.
O sight for the eyes and the ears of the "gods"—
   The crowds, and the bookies declaiming the odds!

LIGHTS

1. 'Twas Tennyson sang of her beauty.
2.   The playwright begins with a tree.
3. To usher in Spring is his duty.
4.   His "belt" is quite easy to see.
5. His dame was a wrong 'un (such eyes and such lips);
   Her special concern? Say, the launching of ships!

• 16 •

UPRIGHTS

In an age when for fiction we frequently look
   To the sex that's supposed to be weak,
When we're told every day some she-novelist's book
   Is a triumph that's almost unique,
Let us take off our hats (as their names we write down)
To two who long since won celebrity's crown.

LIGHTS

1. Here's a gentleman bidding farewell to his steed.
2.   A calling once greatly despised.
3. 'Tis here, so they say, that Bohemians feed.
4.   Both the thing, and the tale, are much prized.
5. More than ever, to climb such a height seems absurd.
6. The peculiar slogan produced by a bird.

ACROSTAGRAMS

• 1 •

UPRIGHTS

This a miser holds to, fast;
That describes the wintry blast.

LIGHTS

1. Poet, let us hear from you.
2. Anagram of uprights two
   (And is *not* much fun).
3. "B—P" loses tail and head.
4. Hither all roads lead, 'tis said.
5.   Here's a slippery one.

• 2 •

UPRIGHTS

When I'm "red" I'm much decried.
I bring you warmth at Christmastide.

LIGHTS

1. You'll seek for me in rustic fields.
2. The fairest flower our woodland yields.
3. A savage cat from foreign clime.
4. Throw out a backward-flowing time.

• 3 •

UPRIGHTS

'Tis here I'll meet you, Mr Sheep.
You raise your voice to call Bo-Peep.

LIGHTS

1. My tale was told by Swift (the Dean).
2.   I stood beneath a chestnut tree.
3. In every club too often seen.
4.   The poet Petrarch sang of me.
5. I play at Bridge, but seldom win,
   For South, the dealer, does me in!

117

• 4 •

UPRIGHTS

I *this* my foe—I *this* him so;
But *that* it was that laid him low!

LIGHTS

1. An expert in infanticide.
2. A love-feast? Or an opening wide?
3. "Great Anna" liked it, all allow.
4. A dizzy height confronts you now.
5. Here scarcity—it might be said—
   Lies hidden in a twisted thread.

• 5 •

UPRIGHTS

He who'd write my *first* all day,
Must my *second*—so they say!

LIGHTS

1. King of Troy long, long ago.
2. Through tropic jungles watch me flow.
3. The King's domain (his wrath refuse),
4. And, to conclude, a tragic muse.

• 6 •

UPRIGHTS

In halls of *this* I dwell, but when
      The skies of spring are blue,
I pack my traps and then, perhaps,
      'Tis *that* I like to do!

LIGHTS

1. An ancient one as wedding guest was seen.
2. Familiar "plant" at Penge or Turnham Green.
3. Turn back, Othello; here there's lots for you.
4. I go off nicely (if "report" be true).
5. Here's M, or N, or B perchance, or P,
6. A dabbler in the "serpentine" was she!

• 7 •

UPRIGHTS

"I sometimes *this*, in accents which
    Or loud or soft can be."
"If loud or soft is what you want,
    You'd best make use of me!"

LIGHTS

1. A symbol of parochial pride.
2.   Though solit'ry, I'm more than one.
3. I'm finished—that's at once descried!
4.   A list of things that should be done.
5. This gentleman, when far from well,
    Planned to take refuge in a cell.

• 8 •

UPRIGHTS

This is bright; transpose, and hence
Find for *that* a consequence.

LIGHTS

1. Hurry, Hans, and bring the beer.
2. Music (of a sort) is here.
3. These bring Hollywood renown.
4. And this was a Mikado's town.
5. The beer returns—a royal affair!
6. Attenuated here the air.

119

• 9 •

UPRIGHTS

A plumber might come back for me.
Eleven of us here you'll see.

LIGHTS

1. I'm on the Free List, if you look.
2. You'll find a fellow in a nook.
3. A faery queen.
4.   Along the track
   Behold a lady "coming back".

• 10 •

UPRIGHTS

A Roman soldier? Use on maps more topical!
Two different trees—one native and one tropical.

LIGHTS

1. At the end of the story, 'tis me you'll espy.
2. Though an integer, headless and tail-less am I.
3. Here's a weaving-machine, or a gull overhead.
4. "Madam, I'm Adam", her palindrome said.
5. In the books they "run out" (which we don't often see)—
   And think of the cattle, by those of the Dee!

• 11 •

UPRIGHTS

I might be "one in the eye",
    A "rip" also;
A heavy burden I—
    Those bearing it know!

LIGHTS

1. I'm nautical—a rodent coming back,
2. And here, of what is puzzling, there's no lack,
3. See, two by two, the animals emerge.
4. The claims of one that's human I would urge.

• 12 •

UPRIGHTS

I'm thrown about, to mark occasions festive.
"Little by little". Pray, is that suggestive?

LIGHTS

1. 'Twas more days work than one, ere I was born.
2.   Between the Bull and Magpie, look for me.
3. A zodiacal beast is "off his corn".
4.   Uncertain in my ways I tend to be.

• 13 •

UPRIGHTS

My keeper is—perchance—a noble lord.
With us (and cakes) adorn the groaning board.

LIGHTS

1. My country's pretty "dry",
2. And hard to grasp am I.
3. Because I'm old, I'm prized.
4. By Wordsworth eulogised.

• 14 •

UPRIGHTS

Nowhere? Yes, he knew it well.
Of brothers twain the legends tell.

LIGHTS

1. Here's Othello, bless his heart.
2. Hence may nuts and wine depart.
3. Dora stands as my defence.
4. Here you—use your common sense.

ANAGRAMS

• 1 •

Five Ordinary Words

1. I'SE FINE BLADE
2. RED BERET, VERA
3. COST IT MITE
4. ANTIDOTES RIPEN
5. BILL, A YUCCA I'LINT

• 2 •

Five More Ordinary Words

1. LAMPS' SPITE
2. COINS A CLOT
3. NEC NOT LATIN
4. BOOR OR I ON CART
5. I COP A COP TUNER

• 3 •

Five Ordinary Words

1. ACID EN NEL
2. ACID IN MEL
3. ACID SIR MEL
4. ACID SENT NEL
5. ACID SENT LCK

• 4 •

Five Famous Novels

1. IF A TRY, IVAN
2. CUPID JAP'D REINDEER
3. M'YES, NOD O'BAND
4. NUN MAY GINGER
5. IF DAVE LICK FOE, WREATH

• 5 •

Five Heroes of Antiquity

1. MOSIS THE CELT
2. LEAN AD REX
3. DIME TAILS
4. CUSS A JAR LIEU
5. SEA CLOUTS CHOIR

• 6 •

Five English Plays

1. POOR SON QUOTES CHEST
2. NAN REMANDS PUMA
3. HAND STOLL FRESH COCOA
4. FLOW THEY OR THAWED
5. HIRE HIM UNSAVOURY MEN

• 7 •

Five Modern Novels

1. VOICE—NAN RAN
2. MAT, LOWER FLARES
3. HASTY GORSE FEAT
4. TEST IN TREES, SIR
5. HELP RAVAGE PER NETS

• 8 •

Five Ordinary Words

1. TED PRICE
2. TED PRICE MAN
3. TED PRICE ULLA
4. TED PRICE UVOR
5. TED PREECE DUNN

DUOGRAMS
(i.e. Anagrams of two words)

• 9 •
European towns
1. WORN BECOS ME
2. ENVIABLER INN
3. MAD DREAM MID STAR
4. GRILL SHAME US, BAR ME
5. INN PLOT STAIN COUNTER

• 10 •
English Towns
1. NORMAN DOLE STENCH
2. INK MAR GRIMY HOB
3. 'S ELEPHANTS' MUD TOO
4. WEE OR RICH STENCIL
5. HIP BULGE BOOTS TERROR

• 11 •
American Cities
1. BONEY WON STORK
2. CATS CONFIDE IRON STAR
3. AH, I SHA'N'T WIN COG-COG
4. UNPOLITE HUMANS' LID
5. CAN-CAN NITRE I' SNOW-LINE

• 12 •
Wild Animals
1. HALF OGRE'S FIT
2. GOT A MILDER LIAR
3. HEM LACE PLANET
4. MARCH I SHUN, O POOR PIE-POTS
5. PADDY, OR RARE MODEL

MISCELLANEOUS

• 1 •

TWO POINTS OF VIEW

I raise your spirits. Take a backward view:
I can raise weightier things than that for you.
Find the two words.

• 2 •

SEPTETTE

(*Composed at the request of "a youngster of 67 years".*)
My house and — is built of —
'Tis proof 'gainst any weather;
We dine off — and then read —,
And then we — together;
She — the cake, I'll — my life,
"A lass amang the heather."

*The seven missing words are all different and all composed of
the same letters.*

• 3 •

TWO POINTS OF VIEW

Seen from in front? I'm full of charm
(I've just come home again):
Seen from behind? Don't take alarm,
But—I'm a source of pain.
Find the two words.

• 4 •

DECAPITATION

My first, tomorrow, "cast" may be;
Behead, and just a boor you'll see;
Behead again: I bat no more;
I'm stumped, perhaps, or leg-before!
Find the three words.

• 5 •

TWO POINTS OF VIEW

In Rome I was no-one, but when I turn round
A sign (or a portent) is instantly found.
Find the two words.

• 6 •

BABY CROSSWORD

1	2	3	4
5			
6			
7			

Across: (1) A wicked fellow emerges from this cave. (5) Seeking whom he may devour. (6) Smile, please! (7) — is — (Kipling).

Down: (1) Good accommodation at the theatre. (2) Home of a very famous monument. (3) Messenger of the gods. (4) Here shed a "tear".

• 7 •

BABY CROSSWORD

I	2	3	4
5			
6			
7			

Across: (1) Found in skins. (5) Garbled name in a hymn-book. (6) A great comedian. (7) Unfamiliar in May.

Down: (1) Slap-up friends. (2) Sign, please. (3) "City of heart breaks." (4) Once was enough.

• 8 •

TWO POINTS OF VIEW

This little play on words the veriest "pup"
　　Can answer if he'll try:
I'm just a common drink, but turn me up,
　　And oh! how royal am I.
　　　　Find the two words.

• 9 •

DECAPITATION

I'm useful, but of course I am a tie;
Behead me and a place in Herts am I.
Behead again; now, Wagner, have a try.
　　　　Find the three words.

• 10 •

DECAPITATION

I won't annoy you: just behead
And find a legal term instead.
Behead once more and then—behold,
You'll seek me when you're tired and old.
Find the three words.

• 11 •

TWO POINTS OF VIEW

I was a mighty city, strong and fair:
Also (reversed) the love they sang of there.
Find the two words.

• 12 •

TWO POINTS OF VIEW

My keeper turned, and, cut in two,
He *thus* and *thus* came into view.
Elucidate.

• 13 •

DECAPITATION

Beware of me! Behead;
Don't look; listen instead.
Behead again, to form
A refuge from the storm.
Find the three words.

• 14 •

DECAPITATION

An obvious aid to locomotion we;
Behead; an aid more primitive there'll be;
Behead again: we're "serpents" from the sea.
Find the three words.

• 15 •

TWO POINTS OF VIEW

A term of argument. But turn me round,
And find what grows (most often) underground.
Find the two words.

• 16 •

DECAPITATION

My meaning? "Stress", I think, conveys the notion;
Behead me: I'm a means of locomotion;
Behead again: My origin's the ocean.
Find the three words.

• 17 •

DECAPITATION

Begin with—oxtail (that's the sort of thing).
Behead me, and you'll find a tragic king.
Behead again. Perhaps I seek—a ring.
Find the three words.

PALINDROMIC WORD-SQUARES

Everyone has heard of the Latin sentence:

SATOR AREPO TENET OPERA ROTAS

which is not only a palindrome but a perfect word-square:

SATOR
AREPO
TENET
OPERA
ROTAS

reading the same backwards, forwards, downwards or upwards.

In connection with the daily puzzles that I publish in the *News Chronicle*, I invited my readers to construct such word-squares in English. The task is not an easy one. I do not think any sentence, worth the name, can be constructed which consists of five words of five letters each. But it is possible to find sentences of twenty-five letters in all which make good palindromic word-squares. Of the examples which follow, three were submitted by *News Chronicle* readers. The remainder are my own.

I have given each example a descriptive heading, to assist the solver to put together sentences of which the meaning is sometimes exiguous.

PROBLEMS

Form Palindromic Word-squares from the following:

(1) Val, though wrathful, was helpful to animals:
    AAAA DD EEEE IIII LLL RR TT VVVV

(2) Mirth prescribed after the Fall:
    EEEEEEEEEEEE LL N RRRR VVVVVV

(3) Father makes a good discovery in the cellar:
    AAAA EEEE N OOOO PP RRRR SS TTTT

(4) Eva, though deranged, comes to no harm:
    AAAA DDDD EEEE IIII LL MM S VVVV

(5) Defence of D.O.R.A.:
    AAAAA DD EEEE NN OOOO RRRR SS TT

CARD PROBLEMS

CARD PROBLEMS

AUCTION AND CONTRACT BRIDGE: CONTRACT WHIST

I

BIDDING PROBLEMS AT CONTRACT BRIDGE

[Adapted, by permission of the publishers, Messrs Faber and Faber, from Hubert Phillips's book, *One Hundred Contract Bridge Hands*.]

• 1 •

Score: Love-all

South deals and bids One Diamond. West passes.

What should North bid, holding:

♠ 10 7   ♥ 10 3   ♦ K 10 6 2   ♣ A K 8 7 5

• 2 •

Score: Game-all

East deals and passes. South bids One Diamond. West passes. North bids One Spade. East passes.

What should South now bid, holding:

♠ 10 3   ♥ A 9 4   ♦ A Q 10 9 5   ♣ 10 6 3

• 3 •

Score: E—W, game; N—S, love

South deals and bids One Heart. West passes.

What should North bid, holding:

♠ Q 5 3   ♥ 5 4 2   ♦ A 9 7   ♣ J 10 5 3

• 4 •
Score: Love-all

South deals and bids One Heart. West passes.

What should North bid, holding:

♠ A J 6   ♥ Q 6   ♦ A 9 8 3   ♣ K 9 6 5

• 5 •
Score: Game-all

West deals, and West, North and East all pass. South bids Two Diamonds. West passes.

What should North now bid, holding:

♠ A 10 4 2   ♥ K Q 9   ♦ 7 6 2   ♣ K 6 4

• 6 •
Score: Game-all

South deals and bids One Spade. West bids Two Diamonds. North passes.

What should East bid, holding:

♠ J 9 7 2   ♥ A   ♦ K 10 7 4   ♣ K Q 6 3

• 7 •
Score: Game-all

South deals and bids One No Trump. West doubles. North passes.

What should East bid, holding:

♠ Q J 5   ♥ K 4   ♦ K Q 5   ♣ 10 9 7 4 2

• 8 •
Score: Game-all

East deals and passes. South bids One Diamond. West doubles. North redoubles, and East bids One Heart.

What should South now bid, holding:

♠ J 10   ♥ Q 10 8 2   ♦ A K 7 5 2   ♣ Q 7

134

II

PROBLEMS OF BIDDING,
ILLUSTRATED BY ACTUAL HANDS FROM
THE CULBERTSON-LENZ MATCH

[Taken, by permission of Mr Ely Culbertson and his publishers, Messrs Faber and Faber, from his book: *Contract for Auction Players*.]

How would you bid the following hands:

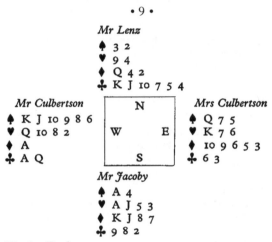

• 9 •

Mr Lenz
♠ 3 2
♥ 9 4
♦ Q 4 2
♣ K J 10 7 5 4

Mr Culbertson
♠ K J 10 9 8 6
♥ Q 10 8 2
♦ A
♣ A Q

Mrs Culbertson
♠ Q 7 5
♥ K 7 6
♦ 10 9 6 5 3
♣ 6 3

Mr Jacoby
♠ A 4
♥ A J 5 3
♦ K J 8 7
♣ 9 8 2

North—Dealer.
Both sides vulnerable.

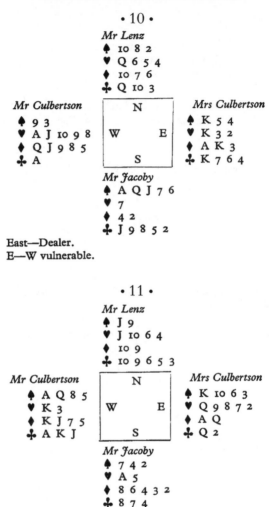

• 10 •

Mr Lenz
♠ 10 8 2
♥ Q 6 5 4
♦ 10 7 6
♣ Q 10 3

Mr Culbertson
♠ 9 3
♥ A J 10 9 8
♦ Q J 9 8 5
♣ A

Mrs Culbertson
♠ K 5 4
♥ K 3 2
♦ A K 3
♣ K 7 6 4

Mr Jacoby
♠ A Q J 7 6
♥ 7
♦ 4 2
♣ J 9 8 5 2

East—Dealer.
E—W vulnerable.

• 11 •

Mr Lenz
♠ J 9
♥ J 10 6 4
♦ 10 9
♣ 10 9 6 5 3

Mr Culbertson
♠ A Q 8 5
♥ K 3
♦ K J 7 5
♣ A K J

Mrs Culbertson
♠ K 10 6 3
♥ Q 9 8 7 2
♦ A Q
♣ Q 2

Mr Jacoby
♠ 7 4 2
♥ A 5
♦ 8 6 4 3 2
♣ 8 7 4

East—Dealer.
E—W vulnerable.

· 12 ·

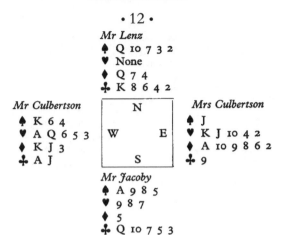

Mr Lenz
♠ Q 10 7 3 2
♥ None
♦ Q 7 4
♣ K 8 6 4 2

Mr Culbertson
♠ K 6 4
♥ A Q 6 5 3
♦ K J 3
♣ A J

Mrs Culbertson
♠ J
♥ K J 10 4 2
♦ A 10 9 8 6 2
♣ 9

Mr Jacoby
♠ A 9 8 5
♥ 9 8 7
♦ 5
♣ Q 10 7 5 3

West—Dealer.
N—S vulnerable.

· 13 ·

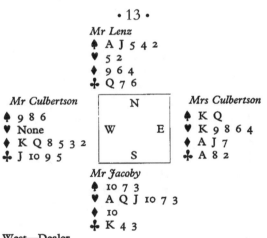

Mr Lenz
♠ A J 5 4 2
♥ 5 2
♦ 9 6 4
♣ Q 7 6

Mr Culbertson
♠ 9 8 6
♥ None
♦ K Q 8 5 3 2
♣ J 10 9 5

Mrs Culbertson
♠ K Q
♥ K 9 8 6 4
♦ A J 7
♣ A 8 2

Mr Jacoby
♠ 10 7 3
♥ A Q J 10 7 3
♦ 10
♣ K 4 3

West—Dealer.
N—S vulnerable.

• 14 •

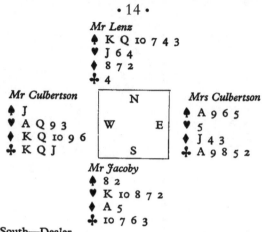

Mr Lenz
♠ K Q 10 7 4 3
♥ J 6 4
♦ 8 7 2
♣ 4

Mr Culbertson
♠ J
♥ A Q 9 3
♦ K Q 10 9 6
♣ K Q J

Mrs Culbertson
♠ A 9 6 5
♥ 5
♦ J 4 3
♣ A 9 8 5 2

Mr Jacoby
♠ 8 2
♥ K 10 8 7 2
♦ A 5
♣ 10 7 6 3

South—Dealer.
Neither side vulnerable.

• 15 •

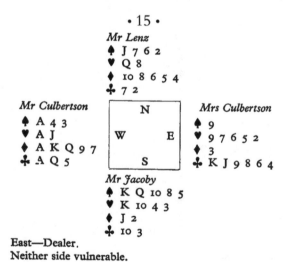

Mr Lenz
♠ J 7 6 2
♥ Q 8
♦ 10 8 6 5 4
♣ 7 2

Mr Culbertson
♠ A 4 3
♥ A J
♦ A K Q 9 7
♣ A Q 5

Mrs Culbertson
♠ 9
♥ 9 7 6 5 2
♦ 3
♣ K J 9 8 6 4

Mr Jacoby
♠ K Q 10 8 5
♥ K 10 4 3
♦ J 2
♣ 10 3

East—Dealer.
Neither side vulnerable.

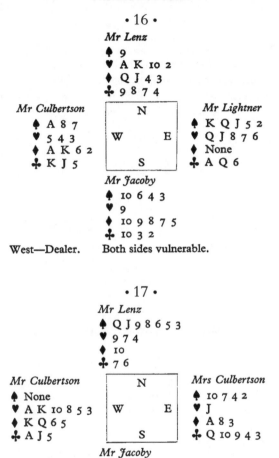

• 16 •

Mr Lenz
♠ 9
♥ A K 10 2
♦ Q J 4 3
♣ 9 8 7 4

Mr Culbertson
♠ A 8 7
♥ 5 4 3
♦ A K 6 2
♣ K J 5

Mr Lightner
♠ K Q J 5 2
♥ Q J 8 7 6
♦ None
♣ A Q 6

Mr Jacoby
♠ 10 6 4 3
♥ 9
♦ 10 9 8 7 5
♣ 10 3 2

West—Dealer.   Both sides vulnerable.

• 17 •

Mr Lenz
♠ Q J 9 8 6 5 3
♥ 9 7 4
♦ 10
♣ 7 6

Mr Culbertson
♠ None
♥ A K 10 8 5 3
♦ K Q 6 5
♣ A J 5

Mrs Culbertson
♠ 10 7 4 2
♥ J
♦ A 8 3
♣ Q 10 9 4 3

Mr Jacoby
♠ A K
♥ Q 6 2
♦ J 9 7 4 2
♣ K 8 2

East—Dealer.   E—W vulnerable.

III

analysed by Ely Culbertson. Reproduced by
special permission of Mr Culbertson and the *Bridge World*.
How should these hands be bid and played?

· 18 ·

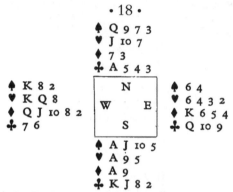

South—Dealer.   East—West vulnerable.

· 19 ·

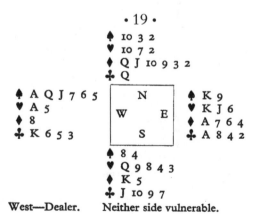

West—Dealer.   Neither side vulnerable.

· 20 ·

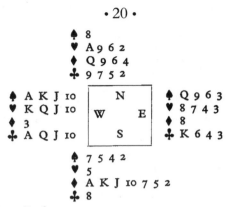

West—Dealer.
Both sides vulnerable.

· 21 ·

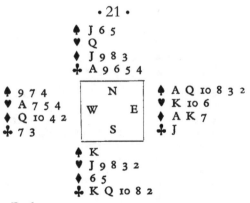

East—Dealer.
Both sides vulnerable.

· 22 ·

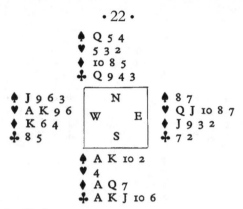

South—Dealer.
Both sides vulnerable.

· 23 ·

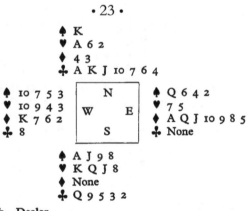

North—Dealer.
North—South vulnerable.

· 24 ·

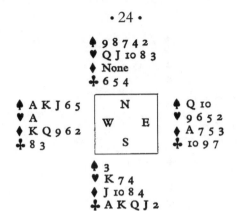

♠ 9 8 7 4 2
♥ Q J 10 8 3
♦ None
♣ 6 5 4

♠ A K J 6 5   ♠ Q 10
♥ A   ♥ 9 6 5 2
♦ K Q 9 6 2   ♦ A 7 5 3
♣ 8 3   ♣ 10 9 7

♠ 3
♥ K 7 4
♦ J 10 8 4
♣ A K Q J 2

West—Dealer.
East—West vulnerable.

· 25 ·

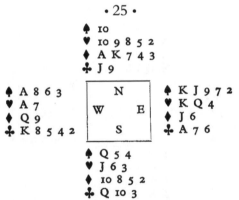

♠ 10
♥ 10 9 8 5 2
♦ A K 7 4 3
♣ J 9

♠ A 8 6 3   ♠ K J 9 7 2
♥ A 7   ♥ K Q 4
♦ Q 9   ♦ J 6
♣ K 8 5 4 2   ♣ A 7 6

♠ Q 5 4
♥ J 6 3
♦ 10 8 5 2
♣ Q 10 3

East—Dealer.
Both sides vulnerable.
If East is Declarer, South must lead ♦ 2.

• 26 •

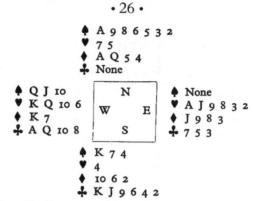

♠ A 9 8 6 5 3 2
♥ 7 5
♦ A Q 5 4
♣ None

♠ Q J 10
♥ K Q 10 6
♦ K 7
♣ A Q 10 8

N
W E
S

♠ None
♥ A J 9 8 3 2
♦ J 9 8 3
♣ 7 5 3

♠ K 7 4
♥ 4
♦ 10 6 2
♣ K J 9 6 4 2

West—Dealer.
Neither side vulnerable.

• 27 •

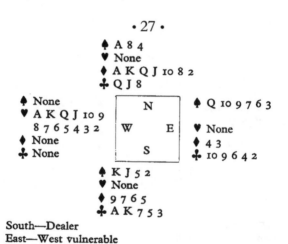

♠ A 8 4
♥ None
♦ A K Q J 10 8 2
♣ Q J 8

♠ None
♥ A K Q J 10 9
    8 7 6 5 4 3 2
♦ None
♣ None

N
W E
S

♠ Q 10 9 7 6 3
♥ None
♦ 4 3
♣ 10 9 6 4 2

♠ K J 5 2
♥ None
♦ 9 7 6 5
♣ A K 7 5 3

South—Dealer
East—West vulnerable

IV

PROBLEMS OF PLAY AT CONTRACT BRIDGE

· 28 ·

[By EDWARD C. WOLFE and CARL T. ROBERTSON.]

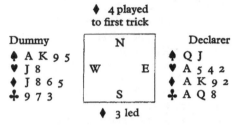

♦ 4 played
to first trick

Dummy	N	Declarer
♠ A K 9 5		♠ Q J
♥ J 8	W E	♥ A 5 4 2
♦ J 8 6 5		♦ A K 9 2
♣ 9 7 3	S	♣ A Q 8

♦ 3 led

Score: Love-all. North deals

The bidding:

North	No Bid	No Bid	No Bid
East	1 ♦	3 N T	
South	No Bid	No Bid	
West	1 ♠	No Bid	

The ♦ 3 is led, the 5 is put up from Dummy, and North drops the 4.

How should East play the hand?

· 29 ·

[Adapted from a well-known Auction Bridge hand.]

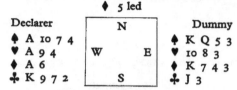

♦ 5 led

Declarer	N	Dummy
♠ A 10 7 4		♠ K Q 5 3
♥ A 9 4	W E	♥ 10 8 3
♦ A 6		♦ K 7 4 3
♣ K 9 7 2	S	♣ J 3

Score: Love-all. West deals

The bidding:

West	1 N T	3 N T
North	No Bid	No Bid
East	2 N T	No Bid
South	No Bid	No Bid

North leads the ♦ 5.

How should West plan the play of the hand?

· 30 ·

[By W. J. BELL.]

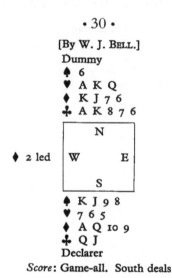

Dummy
♠ 6
♥ A K Q
♦ K J 7 6
♣ A K 8 7 6

♦ 2 led

♠ K J 9 8
♥ 7 6 5
♦ A Q 10 9
♣ Q J
Declarer

Score: Game-all. South deals

The bidding:

South	1 ♦	3 N T	No Bid	No Bid
West	No Bid	No Bid	Double	No Bid
North	3 ♣	6 ♦	Redouble	
East	No Bid	No Bid	No Bid	

[North's redouble is doubtful. A better bid would probably have been six No Trump.]

West leads a small trump.

How should South plan the play of the hand?

· 31 ·

Dummy

♠ Q 10 4
♥ A Q 7 6
♦ 7
♣ A K Q 5 4

♠ K 9 7 3
♥ 5 4 3
♦ 5 3
♣ J 10 6 2

Declarer

Score: Love-all. West deals

The bidding:

West	1 ♦	No Bid	No Bid	No Bid
North	Double	3 ♣	4 ♠	
East	2 ♦	No Bid	No Bid	
South	No Bid	3 ♠	No Bid	

West leads the ♦ K, followed by the ♥ 10.

How should South plan the play of the hand?

· 32 ·

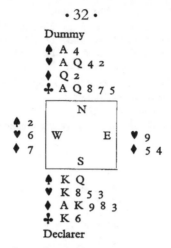

Dummy
♠ A 4
♥ A Q 4 2
♦ Q 2
♣ A Q 8 7 5

♠ 2
♥ 6
♦ 7

♥ 9
♦ 5 4

♠ K Q
♥ K 8 5 3
♦ A K 9 8 3
♣ K 6

Declarer

Score: Love-all. South deals

The bidding:

South	1 ♦	3 ♦	5 ♥	6 N T
West	No Bid	No Bid	No Bid	No Bid
North	3 ♣	3 ♥	6 ♦	No Bid
East	No Bid	No Bid	No Bid	No Bid

The Play

(1) West opens the ♥ 6. The Ace is played from Dummy, the 9 from East, and the 3 from South.

(2) The ♦ Q is led from Dummy. East plays the 4, South the 3 and West the 7.

(3) Dummy plays the ♦ 2, East the 5, and South the Ace. West discards the ♠ 2.

How should South plan to play the remainder of the hand?

• 33 •

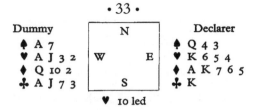

Dummy
♠ A 7
♥ A J 3 2
♦ Q 10 2
♣ A J 7 3

Declarer
♠ Q 4 3
♥ K 6 5 4
♦ A K 7 6 5
♣ K

♥ 10 led

Score: E—W game, N—S love. East deals

The bidding:

East	1 ♦	4 ♥	No Bid
South	No Bid	No Bid	No Bid
West	2 ♥	6 ♦	No Bid
North	No Bid	No Bid	

South leads the ♥ 10.

How should East plan to play the hand?

V

CONTRACT WHIST

PROBLEMS OF BIDDING AND PLAY

[Taken from Hubert Phillips's book on *Contract Whist*, by permission of the publishers, Messrs Faber and Faber.]

NOTE. *Scoring at Contract Whist.* The provisional scoring is as follows:

Points per trick bid and made

4 at No Trump
3 at a suit bid

Points per overtick

2 at No Trump
2 at a suit bid
Game 10 up.

Points per undertrick

10 undoubled
20 doubled
40 redoubled

Bonus for making contract and each overtrick

5 if doubled
10 if redoubled

Bonus for rubber: 50

No slam bonus
No vulnerability
No score for honours

How should the following hands be bid and played?

• 34 •

Score: Love-all. South deals

           ♠ A Q 8 3
           ♥ 4 2
           ♦ 10 9 6
           ♣ Q J 9 2

♠ K 9 4   N   ♠ J 10 7 2
♥ A Q 10 7 6   ♥ 9 8 5
♦ K 7 5   W   E   ♦ J 8 3 2
♣ 10 6   ♣ K 3
                     S

           ♠ 6 5
           ♥ K J 3
           ♦ A Q 4
           ♣ A 8 7 5 4

• 35 •

Score: Game-all. West deals

           ♠ Q 10 6 4 3
           ♥ 9 7 5
           ♦ J 10
           ♣ K 6 3

♠ A 9 7   N   ♠ None
♥ Q 8 4   ♥ J 10 6 3 2
♦ A 9 3 2   W   E   ♦ Q 7
♣ Q J 5   ♣ A 10 8 7 4 2
                     S

           ♠ K J 8 5 2
           ♥ A K
           ♦ K 8 6 5 4
           ♣ 9

• 36 •

Score: Love-all. South deals

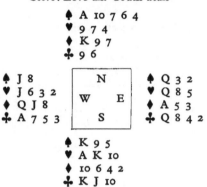

```
                   ♠ A 10 7 6 4
                   ♥ 9 7 4
                   ♦ K 9 7
                   ♣ 9 6

 ♠ J 8            ┌─────────┐      ♠ Q 3 2
 ♥ J 6 3 2        │    N    │      ♥ Q 8 5
 ♦ Q J 8          │ W     E │      ♦ A 5 3
 ♣ A 7 5 3        │    S    │      ♣ Q 8 4 2
                  └─────────┘
                   ♠ K 9 5
                   ♥ A K 10
                   ♦ 10 6 4 2
                   ♣ K J 10
```

• 37 •

Score: N—S 3, E—W love, in the first game. West deals

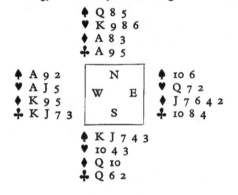

```
                   ♠ Q 8 5
                   ♥ K 9 8 6
                   ♦ A 8 3
                   ♣ A 9 5

 ♠ A 9 2          ┌─────────┐      ♠ 10 6
 ♥ A J 5          │    N    │      ♥ Q 7 2
 ♦ K 9 5          │ W     E │      ♦ J 7 6 4 2
 ♣ K J 7 3        │    S    │      ♣ 10 8 4
                  └─────────┘
                   ♠ K J 7 4 3
                   ♥ 10 4 3
                   ♦ Q 10
                   ♣ Q 6 2
```

· 38 ·

Score: Love-all. East deals

```
                    ♠ Q 4 2
                    ♥ J 8 5 4
                    ♦ 8 4 3 2
                    ♣ 9 4
  ♠ J 10 5      ┌──────────┐      ♠ K 9 7 3
  ♥ Q 10 7      │    N     │      ♥ A 9 2
  ♦ K Q 6 5     │ W      E │      ♦ 9 7
  ♣ A J 8       │    S     │      ♣ Q 10 5 2
                └──────────┘
                    ♠ A 8 6
                    ♥ K 6 3
                    ♦ A J 10
                    ♣ K 7 6 3
```

· 39 ·

Score: Love-all. North deals

```
                    ♠ A 8 6
                    ♥ 9 8
                    ♦ K 7 4 3
                    ♣ K 7 5 2
  ♠ J 10 9 3    ┌──────────┐      ♠ K 7 4 2
  ♥ Q 5         │    N     │      ♥ A 7 4 2
  ♦ A J 8 5 2   │ W      E │      ♦ Q 10 6
  ♣ 10 9        │    S     │      ♣ J 4
                └──────────┘
                    ♠ Q 5
                    ♥ K J 10 6 3
                    ♦ 9
                    ♣ A Q 8 6 3
```

CHESS PROBLEMS

CHESS PROBLEMS

There follows a selection of twenty-four representative Chess Problems, covering the whole field of problem composition. Solvers who desire to explore more thoroughly this fascinating field should study Weenink's admirable treatise, *The Chess Problem*.

• 1 •

By W. GRIMSHAW
Illustrated London News, 1853

BLACK

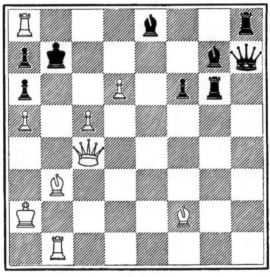

WHITE
White to play and mate in 2

One of the first two-movers to show the germ of a sharp idea. It appeared only in notation, as diagrams were then reserved for longer problems.

• 2 •

By A. F. MACKENZIE
1st prize. *Mirror of American Sports*, 1886

BLACK

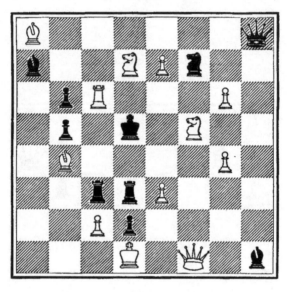

WHITE
White to play and mate in 2

The first two-move masterpiece, and an admirable example of the "waiting-key" style of the last century.

· 3 ·

By G. HEATHCOTE
1st prize. *Hampstead and Highgate Express*, 1905

BLACK

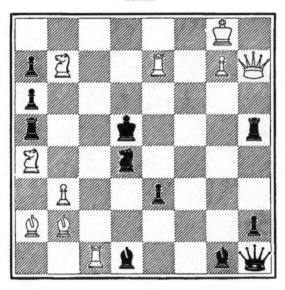

WHITE
White to play and mate in 2

Perhaps the world's most famous two-mover. It is a "task" problem—the generic name used when a specific idea is achieved (in this case, eight variations produced by a black Kt).

• 4 •

By G. GUIDELLI
2nd prize. *L'Eco degli Scacchi*, 1916/17

BLACK

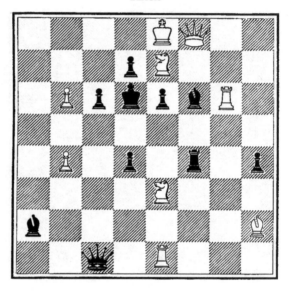

WHITE
White to play and mate in 2

A masterly composition by a young Italian, whose untimely death so shocked the Problem World in 1924. The key is a delightful surprise.

• 5 •

By A. ELLERMAN
1st prize. *Handelsblad*, 1917

BLACK

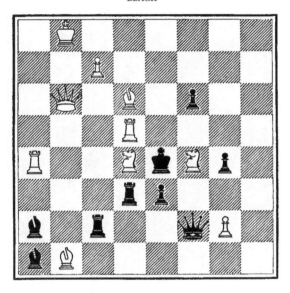

WHITE
White to play and mate in 2

Another bold key-move, introducing two surprisingly complex lines of play. This composer has gained a record number of tourney honours.

• 6 •

By C. MANSFIELD
1st prize. *Good Companion* (U.S.A.) January 1917

BLACK

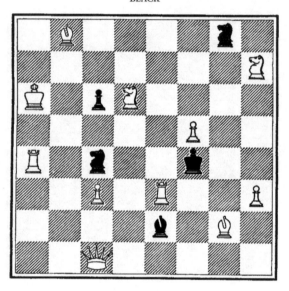

WHITE
White to play and mate in 2

This is generally considered to be the best illustration of the "cross-check" theme (in which the white K is subjected to checks by black).

· 7 ·
By M. NEMEIJER
Tijdschrift N.S.B., 1919

BLACK

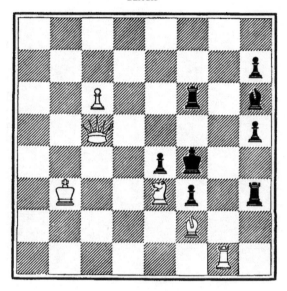

WHITE
White to play and mate in 2

A charming little stratagem. To reveal the nature of the key would rob the solver of genuine enjoyment.

• 8 •

By A. Kraemer
1st prize. *Kockelkorn Memorial Tourney*, 1922

BLACK

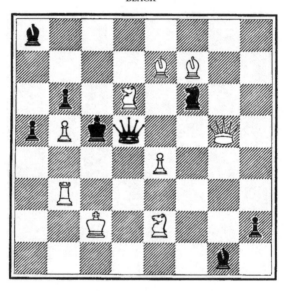

WHITE

White to play and mate in 2

The chivalrous key-move must have formed the inspiration of this problem.

• 9 •

By A. ELLERMAN
1st prize. *Luigi Centurini* (Genoa), 1925

BLACK

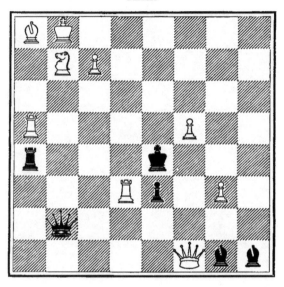

WHITE
White to play and mate in 2

The Ellerman machine has turned out no finer problem than this. One of the very best modern two-movers.

• 10 •

By C. MANSFIELD

1st prize. *El Ajedrez Argentino*, 1926

BLACK

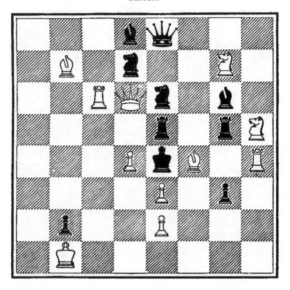

WHITE

White to play and mate in 2

This Argentine tourney attracted 216 competitors, a record since easily surpassed by Budapest.

· 11 ·

By C. Mansfield
1st prize. *British Chess Magazine*, 1930

BLACK

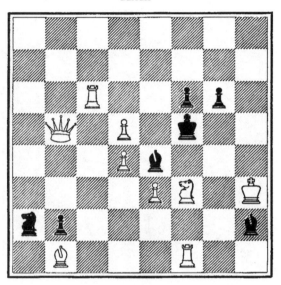

WHITE

White to play and mate in 2

A popular theme to-day is "self-pinning by black". Only two such lines appear above, but they are highly developed and introduced by a "thematic" key.

· 12 ·

By J. A. SCHIFFMANN
1st prize. *Bristol Times and Mirror*, 1927

BLACK

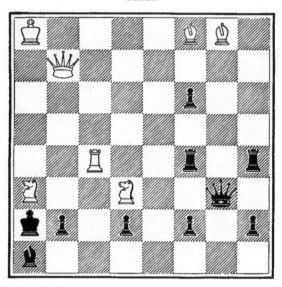

WHITE
White to play and mate in 2

One of the finest keys imaginable. The young Roumanian's death two years ago cut short a brilliant career.

· 13 ·

By J. Fridlizius
1st prize. *St Petersburg Zeitung*, 1898

BLACK

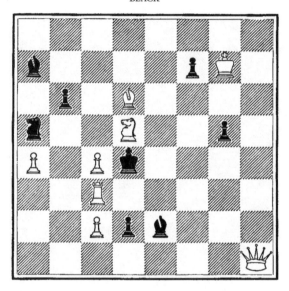

WHITE
White to play and mate in 3

In the best three-movers beauty of mating positions is an essential attribute. Four diverse "model" mates are skilfully combined here.

• 14 •
By G. HEATHCOTE
Reading Observer, 1904

BLACK

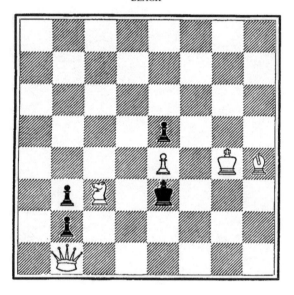

WHITE
White to play and mate in 3

A charming little three-mover constructed with the art that con-ceals art. Two of the four model-mates constitute a pretty "echo".

• 15 •

By O. WURZBURG (after N. HOËG)
Pittsburgh Gazette-Times, 1914

BLACK

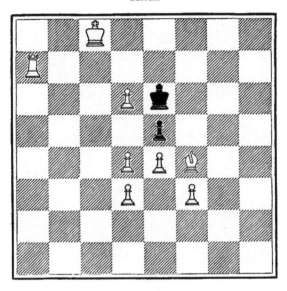

WHITE
White to play and mate in 3

The classic pawn-promotion three-mover. A striking "task" achievement presented with due regard to artistic canons.

• 16 •
By V. Marin
1st prize. *Spanish Tourney*, 1920

BLACK

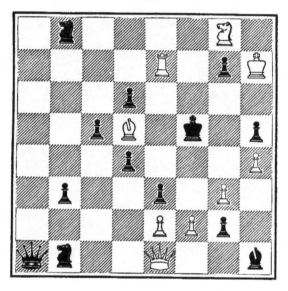

WHITE
White to play and mate in 3

The three-move section would not be complete without a modern specimen combining a sparkling key with quiet strategy and pure mates.

• 17 •

By J. G. CAMPBELL
Illustrated London News, 1868

BLACK

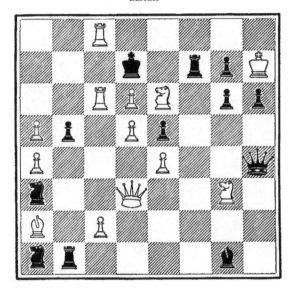

WHITE
White to play and mate in 4

For sheer difficulty this ranks high. Nowadays such stratagems are not tolerated unless combining the requisite degree of artistry.

• 18 •
By H. E. KIDSON
Westminster Club Papers, 1868

BLACK

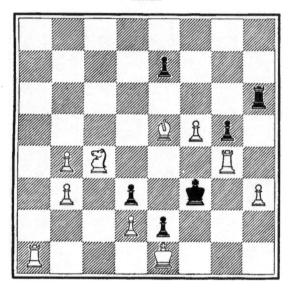

WHITE
White to play and mate in 4

Quite a pleasant old-time conceit. The ultimate use of white's QR is well hidden.

· 19 ·
By W. von HOLZHAUSEN
Deutsches Wochenschach, 1913

BLACK

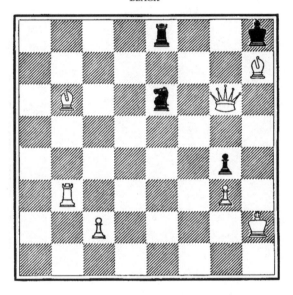

WHITE
White to play and mate in 4

The popularity of four-movers is waning, as they contain few ideas which cannot be expressed in three-move form.

• 20 •
By W. A. Shinkman
Western Advertiser, 1872

BLACK

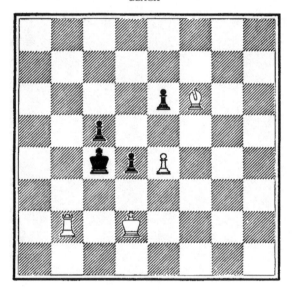

WHITE
White to play and mate in 4

A masterly little four-mover with a definite message. Greater strategy could hardly be exacted from eight pieces.

• 21 •

S. Loyd. *London Era*, 1861 ("Excelsior")

BLACK

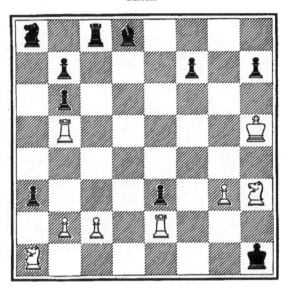

WHITE
White to play and mate in 5

Loyd's only five-mover to justify its existence (in his opinion) originated in a wager. A friend bet him that the white P on QKt2 did not deliver the principal mate. (See solution.)

· 22 ·
By KOHTZ and KOCKELKORN
Schachaufgaben, 1875

BLACK

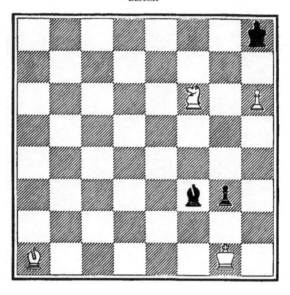

WHITE
White to play and mate in 5

On the surface this looks like an unsound four-mover, as the white B appears to be able to reach KKt 7 four moves hence in a variety of ways. Where is the fallacy?

· 23 ·
By KOHTZ and KOCKELKORN

BLACK

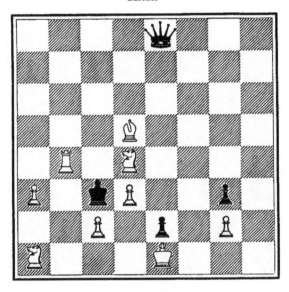

WHITE
White to play and mate in 7

The solution provides a curious duel between the white B and the black Q who has to keep her eye fixed on the two vital squares, Q Kt 4 and K 7, coveted by the white Kt.

• 24 •

By S. LOYD
American Chess Journal, June 1879

BLACK

WHITE

White to play and mate in 50

A curiosity which well repays examination. Its length is by no means a record; a Hungarian specialist recently made a 290-mover!

LORD DUNSANY'S
INFERENTIAL PROBLEMS

· 1 ·

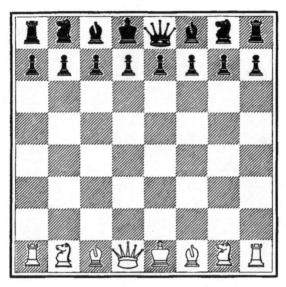

White to play and mate in 4

Lovers of the bizarre will find these creations of Lord Dunsany a welcome departure from the orthodox.

• 2 and 3 •

A

BLACK

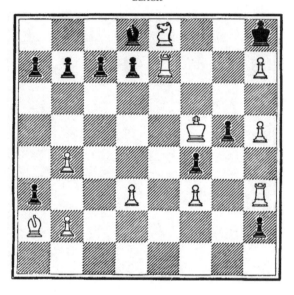

WHITE

In which of the two diagrams on these facing pages (A or B) can White (to play) mate in 2?

For the benefit of beginners it must be explained that all problems must be positions that could arise in actual play.

• 2 and 3 •

B

BLACK

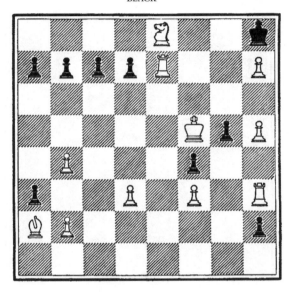

WHITE

When 1 P x P en passant is claimed as a key-move, the legality of this move must be proved.

· 4 ·

BLACK

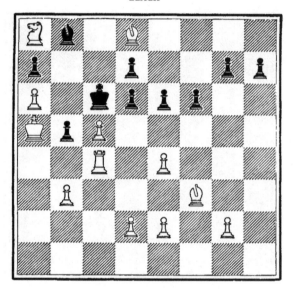

WHITE

White to play and mate in 1

Profound and puzzling retrograde analysis is needed to prove the legality of the key-move. This theme has been worked very fully by T. R. Dawson and W. Hundsdorfer.

· 5 ·

BLACK

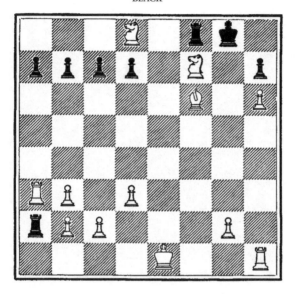

WHITE

It is white to play. Can he castle?

The solver is, of course, required to show whether, in the hypothetical game leading up to this position, the white K and KR could have remained stationary.

· 6 ·

BLACK

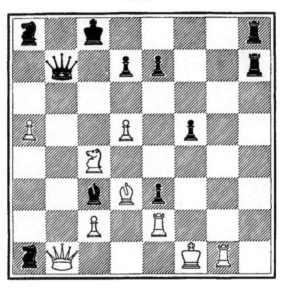

WHITE

White to play and save the game.

This is an end-game, not a "problem", as the conclusion cannot be forced in a specific number of moves; but the strategy used is so bright that it may well conclude this section.

THE
SOLUTIONS

TIME TESTS
OF INTELLIGENCE

SOLUTIONS

• 1 •

Seventeen

• 2 •

The two Americans were husband and wife.

• 3 •

The story is palpably untrue for this reason—that if the Squire had died in his sleep he could not have explained what he was dreaming about.

• 4 •

The counters drawn were: Henry, 6 and 10; Alice, 4 and 7; George, 1 and 3; Mabel, 8 and 9; Lucy, 2 and 5.

• 5 •

The statement is absurd, but not for the reasons given. There are five intervals between the first stroke and the sixth, and six intervals between the sixth and the twelfth.

• 6 •

Only statements (3) and (5) are necessarily true.

• 7 •

Underground.

• 8 •

The Professor had built his house at the North Pole.

• 9 •

Tuesday.

• 10 •

Ptolemy and Ptopsy are wrong.
There cannot be an equilateral right-angled triangle.

• 11 •

The Big Indian was the Little Indian's mother.

• 12 •

The three ingots must weigh 9 lb., 3 lb. and 1 lb.

• 13 •

The two boys had seen one another's faces. Each naturally assumed that his own resembled the other's.

• 14 •

The second and third statements can both be true, but cannot both be false. The first and second can both be false, but cannot both be true.

• 15 •

The shop loses £50, paid over to the swindler Pinchem. (The other £50 he owes them—just as he did before.) As for the £100 refunded to Negus and Co., there is clearly no loss here; since the money would not have been "refunded" if the cheque had not been honoured by the Bank.

• 16 •

The spaces between the letters need readjusting. "O rest a bit, for 'tis a rare place to rest at."

• 17 •

Since Mother bought as many yards of each silk as it cost shillings per yard, her purchase in respect of each silk comes to x^2 shillings, where x is the price in shillings per yard.

But she bought 3 silks, the prices of which were all different; and could have bought three others, the prices of which were different again.

Hence, as Mother (after deduction of discount) received change out of a £5 note, we have to find a number, very little over 100, which is equal to the sums of the squares of two sets of three numbers (all different); the sum of the three numbers being in each case the same.

By experiment, this number is found to be 101.

$$1^2 + 6^2 + 8^2 = 101; 1 + 6 + 8 = 15;$$
$$2^2 + 4^2 + 9^2 = 101; 2 + 4 + 9 = 15.$$

Hence Mother bought silks to the value of £5.1s.0d., and, receiving 2d. in the shilling discount, spent £4.4s.2d.

• 18 •

£12.12s.8d. = 12,128 farthings.

• 19 •

The chances are 12-51 or 13 : 4 against. They are, of course, not affected by the fact that the original pack has been divided.

• 20 •

Mr Cashbox, if he wanted good financial advice, would choose Mr Spoof—although it would cost him more. For, strange as it seems, £10,000 a year rising by £2,000 annually does not yield so lucrative an income as £5,000 half-yearly rising by £500 half-yearly. As witness what Messrs Oof and Spoof would respectively have received:

	Mr Oof	Mr Spoof
First six months	£5,000	£5,000
Second six months	£5,000	£5,500
Total first year	£10,000	£10,500
Third six months	£6,000	£6,000
Fourth six months	£6,000	£6,500
Two years' total	£22,000	£23,000

and so on.

• 21 •

The boy was Georgina's son.

• 22 •

Father is going to Greenfields.

• 23 •

Smith's maid had ascertained (as her question showed) that E was the third letter of Clew's name. There was therefore no point in her asking what E stood for.

Whether this is a sign of lack of intelligence is open to argument, of course. Smith's maid may alternatively have been a humorist; or the victim of a thirst for information.

• 24 •

My son is thirteen.

• 25 •

The proportion of water in the whisky is exactly the same as the proportion of whisky in the water.

• 26 •

If I am selling three small peaches for 1s. and two larger ones for 1s. I can, quite clearly, sell five for 2s. (three small and two large) without losing anything by doing so. But if I have *equal numbers* of large and small ones to begin with, and dispose of them all on the basis of five for 2s., I exhaust my supply of small ones too soon. Our peach-seller, after disposing of ten mixed lots (50 peaches sold for 20s.), would have ten *large* peaches left over, and selling these at five for 2s. he gets 4s. only for them instead of 5s. Hence his loss of 1s. on the whole transaction.

• 27 •

Statements (7), (8) and (9) are *necessarily* true and statement (10) *necessarily* false.

• 28 •

The proportion of *undetected* murders is *ex hypothesi* not known; hence the statistics given could not possibly be formulated.

• 29 •

This is a "catch". "One of the coins" must not be a sixpence —but the other one can be!

• 30 •

One player won 16s. and another 6s. The remaining player lost 32s.

• 31 •

(1) Whistles; (2) Sing; (3) State; (4) Flowers; (5) Guns; (6) Oil; (7) White; (8) Propellers; (9) City; (10) Packs; (11) Petrol; (12) Fly.

· 32 ·

"On the first of July, 1927, I said: 'My brother, who was born on the 15th of June, 1899, was twenty-seven years old last year'."

· 33 ·

(1)	CANADA	(6)	BOLIVIA
(2)	INDIA	(7)	MEXICO
(3)	EGYPT	(8)	PERSIA
(4)	CHINA	(9)	GREECE
(5)	CHILE	(10)	NORWAY

· 34 ·

Poor Mr Wapentake! He thought it had been intended to imply that he smoked a cigar with *a band on*!

· 35 ·

Smith: 15 wickets for 60.
Jones: 20 wickets for 80.

· 36 ·

This problem involves the fundamentals of economic theory, and it is a matter of opinion as to what constitutes the best statement of its solution. The solution published in the *New Statesman and Nation*, towards the end of 1931, was as follows:

"The traveller pays for his own drinks by his exertions in transporting the depreciated dollars to the states where they command their full value. The 'catch' in the puzzle lies in the fact that the currency decrees of the respective states are so stupid as to create an unreal situation. In fact, however, almost the same situation has been created as between Great Britain and Australia, and I read this week that travellers to Australia are bringing home sacks of threepenny-bits."

• 37 •

THE QUEEN AND HER SISTER

If x is the Queen's age, she spends x^3 francs on her purchases. Similarly if y is her sister's age, her sister spends y^3 francs.

Thus $\qquad x^3 - y^3 = 5803.$

Therefore $\quad (x - y)\ (x^2 + xy + y^2) = 5803.$

Hence $\qquad x - y = 7\ (1),$

$$x^2 + xy + y^2 = 829\ (2),$$

since 5803 has no other rational integral factors.

Hence $\qquad x^2 + xy + y^2 = 829\ (2),$

$$x^2 - 2xy + y^2 = 49\ \text{(from 1)}.$$

Therefore $\qquad 3xy = 780,$

$$xy = 260.$$

Therefore $\qquad y = \dfrac{260}{x}$

Whence $\qquad x - \dfrac{260}{x} = 7.$

Therefore $\quad x^2 - 7x - 260 = 0.$

Therefore $\quad (x - 20)\ (x + 13) = 0.$

Therefore $\qquad x = 20\ \text{ or} -13.$

I.e. the Queen is 20.

• 38 •

48 miles.

• 39 •

Brown is the engine-driver.

• 40 •

MISS GREEN'S ALLOWANCE

If x is the number of girls in the school, Miss Green each year gets x^2 pennies given her.

Let X be the number of girls this year.

Let X be the number of girls last year.

Then $\quad\quad\quad\quad X^2 - x^2 = 3091$ (pennies).

Therefore $\quad\quad (X + x)(X - x) = 3091.$

Therefore $\quad\quad\quad\quad X + x = 281,$

$$X - x = 11,$$

for 3091 has no other factors.

Therefore $\quad\quad\quad\quad X = 292/2 = 146.$

I.e. there are 146 *girls in the school.*

• 41 •

The minimum number of journeys is *seven*, as follows:

1. Sambo and Tembo cross.
2. Sambo returns.
3. Sambo and Sir George cross.
4. Sir George returns.
5. Sir George crosses with Jumbo.
6. Sambo returns.
7. Sambo crosses with Limbo.

THE "CALIBAN" PROBLEMS

• 1 •

SLOCOMBE'S BANK

Pickler is eliminated at once, since if he is guilty two of his statements are untrue. This is confirmed by the fact that yet a third statement ("I remember speaking to Dubb") is inconsistent with the innocence of both Dubb and Larkins.

Dubb also is eliminated, since if he is guilty he is "not in any need of money" and thus two of Larkins' statements are false.

This only leaves Larkins, whose guilt is consistent with all the data. The three false statements are:

"I remember speaking to Dubb" (Pickler).

"I was not in the Bank on Thursday" (Larkins).

"I am not in any need of money" (Dubb).

• 2 •

PAUL'S CHRISTMAS PRESENTS

Paul receives presents from Ada, Dorothy, Evelyn, Francis and Grace.

• 3 •

UNITED *v.* VILLA

Since the four teams each play the other three, there are 6 matches in all $(4 \times 3) \div 2$ and hence 12 points in all to be awarded. Now we know that

> United scored 5 points
> Hotspur " 3 "
> Villa " 1 "

whence it follows that Arsenal scored 3 points.

But Arsenal scored no goals at all; therefore they drew all their matches.

We can now construct the framework of our "League Table".

	A.	H.	U.	V.	W.	D.	L.	Points
A.	—	o	o	o	o	3	o	3
H.	o	—	3	4	1	1	1	3
U.	o	4	—	1	2	1	o	5
V.	o	1	o	—	o	1	2	1

Hotspur scored 3 goals against United and yet were beaten; United also beat Villa. They have only 5 goals in all, since 13 were scored altogether and 8 are accounted for above. Hence United beat Hotspur 4–3 and *beat the Villa by* 1 *goal to* 0.

• 4 •

THE BLUE AND RED BALLS

	Bag 1	Bag 2
There were originally	5 B	x R
after 1st transfer	4 B	x R, 1 B

after 2nd transfer $\begin{cases} \text{either } (a) \\ \text{or } \quad (b) \end{cases}$

$$\begin{matrix} 5\text{ B} & x\text{ R} \\ 4\text{ B, }1\text{ R} & (x-1)\text{ R, }1\text{ B} \end{matrix}$$

the chance of (a) being $\dfrac{1}{x+1}$ and of (b) $\dfrac{x}{x+1}$.

After 3rd transfer $\begin{cases} \text{either } (a_1) \\ \text{or } \quad (b_1) \end{cases}$

$$\begin{matrix} 4\text{ B} & x\text{ R, }1\text{ B} \\ 4\text{ B} & x\text{ R, }1\text{ B} \end{matrix}$$

$\quad\quad\quad$ or $\quad (b_2)\quad$ 3 B, 1 R $\quad\quad (x-1)$ R, 2 B

the chance of (a_1) being $\dfrac{1}{x+1}$, of (b_1) $\dfrac{x}{x+1}\cdot\dfrac{1}{5}$, of ($b_2$) $\dfrac{x}{x+1}\cdot\dfrac{4}{5}$.

Thus the chance that there are x R, 1 B in bag 2 is

$$\dfrac{x+5}{5\,(x+1)} \text{ and of } (x-1)\text{ R, 2 B is } \dfrac{4x}{5\,(x+1)}.$$

The chance that a blue ball is now drawn is therefore

$$\frac{x+5}{5(x+1)} \times \frac{1}{(x+1)} + \frac{4x}{5(x+1)} \times \frac{2}{(x+1)} \text{ and this} = \frac{2}{5}.$$

Whence $$9x + 5 = 2(x+1)^2.$$

$$\therefore x = 3.$$

I.e. there were originally three red balls in the bag.

• 5 •

A MILLIONAIRE GIVES ORDERS

Guggelheim's is one of the simplest of cryptographs. The five-letter word groups are first arranged as words of four letters. The message is then read by taking the first letter of the first word, the second letter of the second, and so on:

SARA	DEAR	BOLD	GIRL	TOWN	GOOD	WIDE	
AREA	YOUR	ESAU	KEEP	ERIC	RATS	BEAR	
CATS	ROLL	YARN	OMEN	BOYS	MOTH	EVEN	
SLIM	POLL	MUFF	IVOR	PRAY	DEEM	CORA	
SLOW	ABLE	KEEP	DOGS	TOWN	NOTE	PAST	
WITH	OGRE	PLAY	MADE	NISI	NEAR	AGUE	MOST

which gives the message:

"SELL TODAY SECRETLY MY HELLFIRE ASBESTOS HOLDINGS".

A cryptograph so easily read is hardly worth the trouble expended on it!

• 6 •

DOGS

The owners and dogs are as follows:

Mr Bloodhound owns the Cocker.

Mr Cocker owns the St Bernard.

Mr Mastiff owns the Pom.

Mr Peke owns the Mastiff.

Mr Pom owns the Bloodhound.

Mr Pug owns the Peke.

Mr St Bernard owns the Pug.

Almost any of the clues given can be taken as a starting point for the chain of inferences required.

• 7 •

WHO KILLED POPOFF?

Popoff was killed by Hopkins.

It can easily be ascertained that from Alehouse to Clew is about 30 miles.

Hence to get home in time Hopkins must have got out at Clew; he cannot have been assisted by the car which was put away by 11.35.

How did Hopkins get to Badminster and what part was played by Watt and the car?

The sole explanation which will fit the facts is the following, which can only be arrived at empirically:

Hopkins cycled into Clew; thence he and his bicycle were driven into Badminster in Watt's car. Here Hopkins awaited the train.

Watt motored immediately to Drayton and left the car there. He then cycled back to Clew in time to meet the train. Here Hopkins got out and cycled home, while Watt got in and returned to Clew by car from Drayton.

• 8 •

THE RURITANIAN CABINET

The number of noes given is:

for 8 specified members: 34 $\Big\}$ A
for n additional members: n

It is also the sum of the series

$$0 + 1 + 2 + 3 \ldots,$$

9 terms of which amount to 36.

But this would require 17 members and make $n = 9$, raising A to 43.

Therefore the series must consist of 10 terms, with 19 members; when $n = 11$, and $A = 45$.

I.e. there are 19 ministers in the Cabinet.

• 9 •

INTERROGATORY

Inspector Snooper arrests Sniffwell, whose foolish reference to Puddock's lantern (not mentioned by the police) discloses his knowledge of the circumstances of the crime.

• 10 •

THE SCHOOLGIRL'S CIPHER

There is no clue here, other than the inherent probability that each symbol represents a letter.

To the ingenious solver, however, the character of the symbols, together with the fact that it is a "schoolgirl's" cipher (and therefore probably easy to remember) may suggest a clue. The cipher is as follows:

AB	CD	EF
GH	IJ	KL
MN	OP	QR

Thus A is ⌐; B is ⌐·, and so on.
The message, deciphered, reads:

"HAVE YOU HEARD THAT DEAR OLD FROGGY IS ENGAGED TO A COUNTER JUMPER".

• 11 •

THE NINE DINERS

Number the places at table 1-9 as in the diagram. Put Brown at No. 1. Then there are ladies at 3, 2, 9, 8. Then Mrs Robinson must have been at 5 or 6, for she sits between two men.

(1) Put Mrs Robinson at 5. Then Robinson (sitting next but one) must be at 7. Jones is therefore at 4 and Mrs Jones is at 6 (two places to his left).

But this is not possible, for Mrs Jones sits between her son and daughter and they cannot have been Mr and Mrs Robinson.

(2) Therefore Mrs Robinson is at 6. Then Robinson is at 4, Jones at 7, and Mrs Jones at 9. Smith therefore is at 5, and Miss Jones (next but two to Smith) is either at 2 or at 8. But if Miss Jones is at 8, Mrs Smith is sitting next to Mrs Brown, which is not possible. Therefore Miss Jones is at 2. Then Mrs Smith must be at 8 (since Mrs Jones sits between her son and daughter, who cannot be Mr and Mrs Brown) and Mrs Brown is at 3.

Thus the order is

> 1 Brown
> 2 Miss Jones
> 3 Mrs Brown
> 4 Robinson
> 5 Smith
> 6 Mrs Robinson
> 7 Jones
> 8 Mrs Smith
> 9 Mrs Jones

Note. It follows that Miss Jones is *not* Mrs Jones' daughter. Mrs Jones' daughter is Mrs Smith, and Brown is her son, presumably by a previous husband.

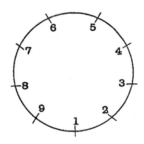

• 12 •

THE FIVE RED BALLS

If there are n balls of which r are red, the probability of drawing 5 red is

$$^rC_5 : {}^nC_5$$
$$= r(r-1)(r-2)(r-3)(r-4)$$
$$: n(n-1)(n-2)(n-3)(n-4),$$

which $= \frac{1}{2}$ only when

$$r = 9, n = 10.$$

I.e. there are *nine* red balls among *ten* balls in the bag.

• 13 •

BETTER THAN BOGEY

To win £25, Spooph must either:

	Win £30 and lose £5
or	" £60 " £35
or	" £90 " £65

No other result is consistent with the data.

But:

(1) In the first case he can win at the most at 5 holes and lose at 1. I.e. he is all square at 12 holes or more.

(2) In the third case he must win at least 8 holes and must lose at least 7. I.e. he cannot be all square at more than 3 holes. Therefore Spooph wins £60 and loses £35.

This means he is 10 strokes up on bogey, at holes which he wins; and 7 strokes down on bogey, at holes which he loses. Therefore Bogey is

$$73 + 3 = 76.$$

• 14 •

THE ACE OF SPADES

(i) In the first drawing, the chance that an Ace is taken $= \dfrac{1}{51}$.

Therefore the chance that B now contains one Ace is $\dfrac{50}{51}$; two Aces $\dfrac{1}{51}$.

(ii) After the second drawing, the chance that C contains two Aces is

$$\frac{50}{51} \cdot \frac{1}{52} + \frac{1}{51} \cdot \frac{2}{52} = \frac{1}{51}.$$

The chance that C contains two Aces is

$$\frac{1}{51} \cdot \frac{50}{52} + \frac{50}{51} \cdot \frac{51}{52} = \frac{50}{51}.$$

(iii) After the last draw, the chance that C contains:

no Ace is $\quad \dfrac{50}{51} \cdot \dfrac{1}{53}$

one Ace is $\quad \dfrac{50}{51} \cdot \dfrac{52}{53} + \dfrac{1}{51} \cdot \dfrac{2}{53}$

two Aces is $\quad \dfrac{1}{51} \cdot \dfrac{51}{53}$

Therefore the chance that Ace is top card is

$$\frac{1}{52} \left[\frac{50}{51} \cdot \frac{52}{53} + \frac{1}{51} \cdot \frac{2}{53} \right] + \frac{2}{52} \left[\frac{1}{51} \cdot \frac{51}{53} \right]$$

$$= \frac{52}{51. \, 53}.$$

• 15 •

"E TENEBRIS LUX"

The mottoes underneath the shields should help towards their interpretation. The first shield is a key to the cipher; the second is the message.

The first shield is divided into 32 sections. Six of these however are duplicates; this leaves 26—the letters of the alphabet!

They are read straight across, beginning at the top left-hand corner. Thus the blank section (occurring 5 times in the 32 sections of the right-hand shield) represents E.

The message reads:

"LEAVE AT ONCE THE YARD HAS YOUR DOSSIER".

• 16 •

MURDER OF DR ZBYSCO

Problems of this type call for (1) correct inference, and (2) evaluation of probabilities. The fantastic or wildly improbable must be rejected (e.g. the passage of Mr Pusch from one moving train to another, or the stabbing of Dr Zbysco, at the window of a moving train, by someone stationed at the window of a train moving in the opposite direction) if reasonably probable solutions are available. Also, solutions are inadmissible which assume circumstances, not set out in the statement of the problem, that would be necessary to the solution—e.g. that Zbysco's train and Pusch's stopped opposite to one another.

Dr Zbysco was stabbed by Borer in the latter's car, outside Botherham station, between 11.10 and 11.14 p.m. His body was put back in the train at Clutter, probably with the connivance of Pocombe and of Pusch. Given a dark night and a wayside station, this feat would present no special difficulty.

• 17 •

MATES

Experiment will show that, to comply with the data, the table of match results must be as follows:

Player	C.	A.	St.	Sp.	M'B.	M.	Sn.	A.	T.	P.	Pts.
1. Casabianca	–	½	½	½	½	I	I	I	I	I	7
2. Alasker	½	–	½	½	½	½	I	I	I	I	6½
3. Steinisch	½	½	–	½	½	½	½	I	I	I	6
4. Spilsbury	½	½	½	–	½	½	½	½	I	I	5½
5. M'Bang M'Wang	½	½	½	½	–	½	½	½	½	I	5
6. Morfew	o	½	½	½	½	–	½	½	½	½	4
7. Snooper	o	o	½	½	½	½	–	½	½	½	3½
8. Algonquin	o	o	o	½	½	½	½	–	½	½	3
9. Titterdown	o	o	o	o	½	½	½	½	–	½	2½
10. Puschowski	o	o	o	o	o	½	½	½	½	–	2

The required results can be read at sight from the table.

• 18 •

THE UTOPIAN LEAGUE

This is distinctly a more difficult puzzle than "United *v.* Villa".

Since 6 teams each play 5 others, the total number of matches is $\frac{6 \times 5}{2} = 15$, and the total number of points divided is 30. Now 4 teams score the same number of points, while the bottom team, had they scored two points more, would have gone to the top.

Hence the points scored must have been:

City   6
Spurs
Villa
Arsenal   } 5
United
Rovers   4

No other distribution of points conforms with the data.

Hence the Rovers had 4 goal-less draws, and, since the City scored all their goals against the Rovers, they had 4 goal-less draws too.

| | | C. | S. | V. | A. | U. | R. | W. | D. | L. | P. | Goals | |
												F.	A.
1.	City	—	o	o	o	o	3	1	4	0	6	3	0
2.	Spurs	o	—				o				5		
3.	Villa	o		—			o				5		
4.	Arsenal	o			—		o				5		
5.	United	o				—	o				5		
6.	Rovers	o	o	o	o	o	—	o	4	1	4	0	3

The above shows what is so far known. What we now have to do is to resolve the "inner table" bounded by the thick line.

Within this framework, each of 4 teams has scored 3 points and *each has a different goal average*, since each has a distinctive place in the table.

There are seven goals to be accounted for, and we know that the Villa beat the Spurs by 1 goal to 0.

The answer can only be found empirically. Only one combination of scores will produce the desired result:

	S.	V.	A.	U.	Goals	
					F.	A.
S.	—	o	3	o	3	I
V.	I	—	o	o	I	I
A.	o	o	—	2	2	3
U.	o	I	o	—	I	2

[Note. The position of these teams is determined by *goal average*, i.e. the ratio of goals scored *for* a team to goals scored *against* it.]

Thus Arsenal beat the United by 2 goals to 0.

• 19 •

SIX AUTHORS IN SEARCH OF A CHARACTER

Mr Brown is sitting in a *centre* seat (between the Essayist and the Humorist) and is obviously neither of these, nor is he the Historian (who is opposite the Essayist) nor the Novelist (who is his brother-in-law).

Mr Brown is therefore either Playwright or Poet.

(1) Assume he is the Playwright and build up the diagram accordingly:

Green, Humorist	Black, Novelist
Brown, Playwright	White, Poet
Pink, Essayist	Gray, Historian

Then Pink (next to Playwright) must be *either* Essayist *or* Humorist: and, since he is reading a book by the Humorist, he must be the Essayist.

Then Green must be the Humorist; for Green is facing the Novelist, and therefore cannot sit in any of the seats opposite.

Gray must be the Historian, for he is reading a book by the author opposite, and we know that Pink is reading Humour and Green is reading Plays.

Whence Black (in the other corner seat) is the Novelist and therefore White is the Poet.

But this solution is inconsistent with the data. For it means that Black and Gray are now both reading Essays, and this is not possible; since six different types of book are being read.

Hence Brown cannot be the Playwright and therefore Brown is the Poet.

(2) We can now reconstruct our plan on a sure foundation:

Essayist	Pink, Historian
Brown, Poet	Playwright
Green, Humorist	Black, Novelist

Brown is the Poet, seated between Essayist and Humorist. The Historian is opposite the Essayist.

Green (facing the Novelist) must be the Humorist, and Black must be the Novelist, since Black is in a corner seat, is reading Essays (and is therefore not the Essayist) and has no interest in History.

Hence the Playwright occupies the other centre seat, and Pink (next to him) is the Historian.

The Playwright therefore is either White or Gray.

Let him be White.

Then the Essayist is Gray.

Then Gray is reading History (since he is reading a book by the author opposite); and, since Pink is reading Humour; Green, Plays; and Black, Essays; and since Brown the Poet can therefore only be reading Fiction, White must be reading Poems.

But White never reads Poetry.

Therefore, the Playwright is Gray, and White is the Essayist.

Hence the six authors are:

> Black, Novelist;
> Brown, Poet;
> Gray, Playwright;
> Green, Humorist;
> Pink, Historian;
> White, Essayist.

• 20 •

BETTY'S CIPHER

GEORGIE PORGIE PUDDING AND PIE
HAS GOT A COLD AND P'RAPS WILL DIE
WHILE SHE'S AWAY HER THANKLESS JOB
WILL BE PERFORMED BY GINGER NOB.

There are rather limited data for a frontal attack on the cipher. The clue is that Betty's mistress *must* have been called "Georgie Porgie". By substitution of letters on this basis sufficient material is obtained to enable the rest of the cipher to be guessed quite easily.

• 21 •

THE EARLY ENGLISH LEAGUE

1. At the end of the *first* round each of the six teams has already a distinctive place in the table. This means (*a*) that no match was drawn, (*b*) that a different score resulted in each of the three matches played.

2. Every team scored in these three matches. Therefore at least 12 goals were scored, since the minimum scores consistent with this result are:

> 3-1 in one match;
>
> 2-1 in a second match;
>
> 3-2 in a third match.

And since two teams each scored two goals, this is the only distribution of goals in these three matches which leaves as many as four goals available for the other 4 rounds.

3. Now 4 goals are required for the other 4 rounds. For we can deduce from the data given:

> (1) that the Normans won their second round match;
>
> (2) that the Angles won a match in their second or third round;
>
> (3) that the Britons won two matches after the first round.

4. Hence we know for certain that the results of the first round are:

> Britons 3,   Saxons 1;
>
> Normans 2,   Angles 1;
>
> Danes 3,   Jutes 2;

and that as regards subsequent matches four resulted in wins of 1-0, the winners being the Britons (2), the Normans (1) and the Angles (1), and the losers the Jutes (2) and the Danes (2), while the remainder were goal-less draws.

5. The final competition table can be built up from the above data:

	Team	Matches			Goals		Points
		W.	D.	L.	F.	A.	
I.	Britons	3	2	—	5	I	8
2.	Normans	2	3	—	3	I	7
3.	Angles	I	3	I	2	2	5
4.	Danes	I	2	2	3	4	4
5.	Saxons	—	4	I	I	3	4
6.	Jutes	—	2	3	2	5	2

• 22 •

MR SOUTH

Mr South is not sitting South [*ex hypoth.*]. Therefore he is N., E. or W.

(1) Suppose Mr South sits N.

Then he is 6 down on his contract.

Then (*a*) his partner cannot be Mr West for with Mr West as his partner Mr South could not possibly go down 6;

(*b*) his partner cannot be Mr North for in this case either two players or none would be sitting in their appropriate seats;

(*c*) his partner cannot be Mr East for in this case Mr West must have doubled the hand; and Mr West must be sitting West and therefore cannot speak.

Therefore Mr South is not sitting N.

(2) Suppose Mr South is sitting E.

Then (*a*) his partner cannot be Mr West for if so Mr South bids three spades unsupported by his partner and still goes down 4;

(*b*) his partner cannot be Mr East for if so Mr North sits North and cannot bid;

(*c*) his partner cannot be Mr North for if so no player is in his appropriate seat.

Therefore Mr South sits W.

Whence it is obvious that Mr East is Mr South's partner; the position being

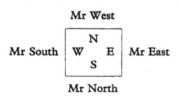

212

The hands and bidding were:

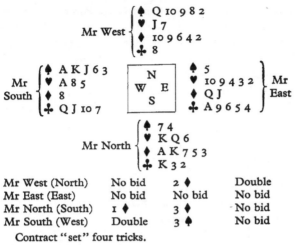

	Mr West			Mr North	

Mr West (North)	No bid	2 ♦	Double
Mr East (East)	No bid	No bid	No bid
Mr North (South)	1 ♦	3 ♦	No bid
Mr South (West)	Double	3 ♠	No bid

Contract "set" four tricks.

· 23 ·

OPEN-TOP BUSES

The solution of this problem is as follows. Evidently 20 buses are needed for the service. In the morning Mr Brown has seen every bus from the first bus to pass Piccadilly Circus after 10.15 a.m. (the 9 a.m. from Coulsdon at 10.20 a.m., No. 1) to the last bus to pass South Croydon before 11.15 a.m. (the 10.50 a.m. from Coulsdon at 11.10 a.m., No. 12). Of these, Nos. 3 and 12 are open-top buses.

In the evening Mr Brown has seen every bus from the first bus to pass South Croydon after 7.50 (the 6.40 p.m. from Camden Town at 7.55 p.m.) to the last bus to pass Piccadilly Circus before 8.50 p.m. (the 8.30 p.m. from Camden Town at 8.45 p.m.). The former bus is the one that worked the 6.40 p.m. from Camden Town, the 5 p.m. from Coulsdon, the 3.20 p.m. from Camden Town, the 1.40 p.m. from Coulsdon, the 12 noon from Camden Town, the 10.20 a.m. from Coulsdon and is therefore No. 9. Similarly the latter bus is No. 20. Of this group of buses, Nos. 9, 10 and 11 are known already to be covered-top. No. 12 is known to be an open-top and the only three among Nos. 9–20 are three in succession, including No. 12. They cannot be Nos. 10, 11, 12 nor Nos. 11, 12, 13, as at least one in each case is known to be covered-top. They must therefore be Nos. 12, 13, 14.

Thus there are four open-top buses on the service, Nos. 3, 12, 13 and 14.

• 24 •

THE PROFESSOR'S DAUGHTERS

The solution can be arrived at by trial and error.*

Let N be the number of daughters.

Then each buys N presents.

* There is a mathematical solution in which the element of trial and error enters to only a light extent.

If there are N daughters there are N purchasers but there are $N + 1$ different ways in which the choice of presents at different prices may be made at any one stall, e.g. if the prices were x and y the amounts spent by any one girl might be Nx, $(N - 1) x + y$, $(N - 2) x + 2 y$, ... Ny. The total of these is $\frac{1}{2}N (N + 1) (x + y)$ and exceeds 89 by one of the numbers which go to make up the total.

If $N = 7$, $\frac{1}{2}N (N + 1) = 28$. Therefore $(x + y) = 4$ and the number to be added to 89 is 23 which is greater than any of the numbers $7x$, $6x + y$, etc., as x and y are less than 4. Thus 7 is impossible.

If $N = 6$, $\frac{1}{2}N (N + 1) = 21$. Therefore $(x + y) = 5$ and the number to be added to 89 is 16 so that if $x = 2$, $y = 3$, $16 = 4y + 2x$; but if $x = 1$ and $y = 4$ we have the equation

$$16 = (N - a) x + ay = 6x + a (y - x) = 6 + a.3,$$
and there is no integral solution.

If $N = 5$, $\frac{1}{2}N (N + 1) = 15$. Therefore $x + y = 7$ and again 89 + 16 = 105.

If $x = 2$, $y = 5$, $16 = (N - a) x + ay = 10 + a.3$. ∴ $a = 2$,

$x = 3$, $y = 4$, $16 = (N - a) x + ay = 15 + a$. ∴ $a = 1$.

Thus there are two solutions for $N = 5$ but one only for $N = 6$. Any other value for N can easily be shown (as in the case of $N = 7$) to be impossible.

Hence N is such a number that $\Sigma_N (xA + yB)$, where $x + y = N$ and A and B are different numbers, neither greater than 5, is equal to 89.

It is at once clear that N must be greater than 4 and less than 8, since in the former case at the most 74s. could be spent; in the latter, at least 92s.

Hence N can only be 5, 6 or 7.

Experiment shows that N might in fact be 5, and the prices at the stall selected 5s. and 2s.;

or 5, and the prices at the stall selected 4s. and 3s.;

or 6, and the prices at the stall selected 3s. and 2s.

It cannot be 7.

But since the Professor knew there could be no option as to the stall selected, the solution 5 is inadmissible.

I.e. the Professor had SIX *daughters*.

• 25 •

NEWS FROM A SPY

Zymenoff is using a simple cryptograph. Analysis of his letters gives the following result:

(1)	E	17 (1)		(7)	I	11 (5)
(2)	{R	14 (8)		(8)	A	10 (3)
	{N	14 (6)		(9)	{D	7 (10)
(4)	{S	13 (7)			{L	7 (11)
	{O	13 (4)			{U	7 (12)
(6)	T	12 (2)			{F	7 (15)

The second set of figures in brackets give the corresponding positions in the frequency table. From this it is fairly evident that no cipher has been used; all we have to do is to re-arrange the letters.

Various possibilities will suggest themselves. In fact, the heading "Code 10" supplies the clue. There are 160 letters in all. Try arranging these in 16 groups of ten. This gives the following result:

```
T B T N R          O E S A M
R L T D N          R R W N I
A E O R I          T S I D D
N L D E N          E F L T N
S E A D E          D O L O I
P A Y I I          F U P M G
O V E N N          O R A O H
R E I F C          U S S R T
T S G A H          R U S R Z
I E H N G          D B S O Y
N A T T U          E M E W M
F S E R N          S A A A E
L T E Y S          T R L B N
E P N F E          R I I O O
X O H O S          O N S U F
I R U U C          Y E L T F
```

The message (read downwards) is now "sticking out a yard". It reads:

"TRANSPORT 'INFLEXIBLE' LEAVES EASTPORT TO-DAY; 1800 INFANTRY, FOUR NINE INCH GUNS; ESCORTED FOUR DESTROYERS, FOUR SUBMARINES. WILL PASS SEAL ISLAND TO-MORROW ABOUT MIDNIGHT. ZYMENOFF".

• 26 •

COLONEL BLOTTO

(1) The distribution of the enemy's forces is not known. It is therefore equally probable that any enemy unit is in any one of the four fortresses. Hence there are 4^3 or 64 possible enemy distributions:

In	4 of these the units are distributed				...	3 0 0 0
"	36	"	"	"	"	... 2 1 0 0
"	24	"	"	"	"	... 1 1 1 0

(2) Now, the Colonel has 5 possible distributions of his 4 units.

4	0	0	0
3	1	0	0
2	2	0	0
2	1	1	0
1	1	1	1

We have to consider the relative effectiveness of each of these, in respect of each possible enemy distribution.

(3) Take, for example, the distribution, 2 2 0 0:   Total
  (i) Against the enemy distribution 3 0 0 0:   points
    Blotto will in 2 cases *lose* 2 points   ...   – 4
      "   " 2 cases gain 1 point   ...   + 2
  (ii) Against the distribution 2 1 0 0:
    Blotto will in 6 cases gain 2 points   ...   +12
      "   " 12   "   1 point   ...   +12
      "   " 18 cases neither gain nor lose   —
  (iii) Against the distribution 1 1 1 0:
    Blotto will in 18 cases gain 3 points   ...   +54
      "   " 6   "   1 point   ...   + 6
                    Total gain ...   + 82

Hence in this case Blotto's expectation is $\dfrac{82}{64}$ points and the chance that he will be outpointed is $\dfrac{2}{64}$ or 31 to 1 against.

(4) Similar calculations will show that Blotto distributing his forces

2	1	1	0	will stand to gain	$\frac{55}{64}$ points.
3	1	0	0	" "	$\frac{41}{64}$ "
1	1	1	1	" "	$\frac{28}{64}$ "
4	0	0	0	" "	$\frac{1}{64}$ "

Hence the 2 2 0 0 distribution is on balance the most advantageous.

Blotto should choose at random two of the enemy fortresses and send two of his units against each.

• 27 •
FAMILY BRIDGE

Robinson plays with his daughter.

This is either Mrs Smith, Mrs Brown or Mrs Jones.

(1) Let Robinson's daughter be Mrs Smith. Then they must be playing against Smith and Mrs Robinson. Then at the other table Jones is partnering his sister (Mrs Brown) who therefore is Brown's mother. This is impossible.

Therefore Robinson's daughter is not Mrs Smith.

(2) Let Robinson's daughter be Mrs Brown. Then Smith's partner is Mrs Robinson or Mrs Jones.

    (a) Let Smith's partner be Mrs Robinson. Then Jones' partner is Mrs Smith, and Mrs Brown's partner is Mrs Jones.

    Then (i) if Mrs Smith and Mrs Jones are playing against one another, each is the other's mother!

        (ii) if Mrs Jones and Mrs Brown are playing against one another, Brown's wife is his mother!

218

(iii) if Mrs Jones and Mrs Robinson are playing against one another, Brown and his wife have the same mother!

Therefore Smith's partner cannot be Mrs Robinson.

(b) Let Smith's partner be Mrs Jones. Then Brown's partner is Mrs Smith or Mrs Robinson.

(i) Let Brown's partner be Mrs Smith. Then Jones' partner is Mrs Robinson.

Not possible, as no player's uncle is participating.

(ii) Let Brown's partner be Mrs Robinson.

Not possible, as Mrs Brown would have married her mother's brother.

Therefore Robinson's daughter cannot be Mrs Brown.

Therefore Robinson's daughter (and partner) is Mrs Jones.

Jones' sister (and partner) cannot be Mrs Robinson [*supra*] and therefore is either Mrs Brown or Mrs Smith.

Let Jones' partner be Mrs Smith. Then Smith's partner is Mrs Brown.

Then (i) Brown plays against Mrs Brown (not possible);

or   (ii) Mrs Robinson is the mother of both Mr and Mrs Jones;

or   (iii) Mrs Robinson is her own daughter's daughter!

Therefore Jones' partner is Mrs Brown.

Therefore Smith's partner is Mrs Robinson and Brown's partner is Mrs Smith.

And they must be seated as follows:

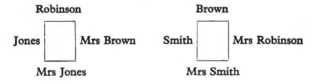

219

• 28 •

RAIN

The brothers had 14 wet days between them and each had 2 fine days. Either, one had 8 wet days and the other 6; or, they had 7 wet ones each. We can find out, first, what the relevant combinations of wet and fine days were.★

	I *a*. 8 wet days				£
(1) 8 consecutive wet days					36 – 2 = 34
(2) Wet spells of 7 days and 1 day					29 – 2 = 27
(3) " "	6	"	2 days		24 – 2 = 22
(4) " "	5	"	3 "		21 – 2 = 19
(5) " "	4	"	4 "		20 – 2 = 18
(6) " "	6	"	1 and 1		23 – 2 = 21
(7) " "	3	"	2 " 1		19 – 2 = 17
(8) " "	4	"	2 " 2		16 – 2 = 14
(9) " "	4	"	3 " 1		17 – 2 = 15
(10) " "	3	"	3 " 2		15 – 2 = 13

	I *b*. 6 wet days				£
(11) 6 consecutive wet days					21 – 4 = 17
(12) Wet spells of 5 days and 1 day					16 – 4 = 12
(13) " "	4	"	2 days		13 – 4 = 9
(14) " "	3	"	3 "		12 – 4 = 8
(15) " "	4	"	1 and 1		12 – 4 = 8
(16) " "	3	"	2 " 1		10 – 4 = 6
(17) " "	2	"	2 " 2		9 – 4 = 5
(18) " "	3	"	1, " 1 and 1		9 – 4 = 5
(19) " "	2	"	2 " 1 " 1		8 – 4 = 4
(20) " "	2	"	1, 1, 1 and 1		7 – 4 = 3

	II. 7 wet days				£
(21) 7 consecutive wet days					28 – 3 = 25
(22) Wet spells of 6 days and 1 day					22 – 3 = 19
(23) " "	5	"	2 days		18 – 3 = 15
(24) " "	4	"	3 "		16 – 3 = 13
(25) " "	5	"	1 and 1		17 – 3 = 14
(26) " "	4	"	2 " 1		14 – 3 = 11
(27) " "	3	"	2 " 2		12 – 3 = 9
(28) " "	4	"	1, 1 and 1		13 – 3 = 10
(29) " "	3	"	2, 1 " 1		11 – 3 = 8
(30) " "	2	"	2, 2 " 1		10 – 3 = 7

Hence, to get a difference of £11 in the two payments, the relevant payments must be one of the following combinations:

1. (4) and (14)	5. (9) and (19)
2. (4) and (15)	6. (21) " (25)
3. (7) " (16)	7. (22) " (29)
4. (8) " (20)	

but it will be found that, of these, only Nos. 1 and 2 satisfy the data (i.e. that in each case the first and seventh days were fine). Nos. 4 and 5 are all invalidated by the fact that arrangements (7), (8), (9) all demand a wet day to begin with. No. 6, by the fact that in arrangement (21) the seven wet days are consecutive. No. 7 by the fact that arrangement (22) demands six consecutive wet days. Whereas, between Nos. 1 and 2 it is a matter of indifference which arrangement of wet and fine days occurs.

Hence Jones received £8 and his brother £19; between them, £27.

* By no means all the data that follow are necessary to the solution of this problem. I have set out the figures in full, however, as the reader may find it interesting to construct other problems from them.

• 29 •

THE MAD MILLIONAIRES

(1) *Blosheim's chances.*

His chance of *not* getting married is easily calculated; his chance of getting married can then be ascertained by subtracting the former chance from unity.

Blosheim can only fail to get married if he guesses wrong six times running.

Now each night there is one chance in six that he will guess wrong. Hence his chance of *not* getting married is 5/6.

Hence for the six nights his chance of *not* getting married is

$$\frac{5^6}{6^6} = \frac{15625}{46656}$$

Whence by subtraction his chance of getting married

$$= \frac{31031}{46656}$$

(2) *Blum's chances.*

His chance of failure on the first night is $^4/_5$

        "   "   "   second   " $^3/_4$

        "   "   "   third   " $^2/_3$

His chance of complete failure is thus

$$^4/_5 \cdot {}^3/_4 \cdot {}^2/_3 = {}^2/_5.$$

Hence Blum's chance of getting married $= {}^3/_5$.

It is thus clear

(1) that Blosheim has the better chance of getting married.

(2) That the chance that both millionaires will remain bachelors

$$= \frac{15625}{46656} \cdot \frac{2}{5}$$

$$= \frac{3125}{23328}$$

• 30 •

PUSCHOVSKI

This is really a comparatively simple cipher. If the last digit of each (alleged) page number is removed, we get:

16, 9, 3, 3, 1, 4, 9, 12, 12, 25, and so on.

Taking the 16th, 9th, 3rd, 3rd, etc., letters of the alphabet we then get the message:

PICCADILLY CIRCUS NINE TO-NIGHT.

Once this solution is discovered, its correctness is, of course, beyond question, as the odds against such a message occurring fortuitously are incalculable.

• 31 •

PLUTOCRATS AT PLAY

This problem can only be solved empirically. The solution turns on the calculation of Goldstein's lead at the thirteenth hole. It will be found (by experiment) that Goldstein must have been 4 up at the thirteenth, having lost the 1st, 3rd and 4th; halved the 2nd, 5th and 10th, and won the remainder. Hence he was 6 up at the 15th. Thus he won £21 on each of the last 3 holes (£63 on the three), whereas, had Snagg won them, he (Goldstein) would on these three holes have been only £31 up; and thus the three missed putts cost Snagg £32.

• 32 •

FUN ON THE 'PHLEGMATIC'

(1) One point is awarded in respect of each conundrum set, and, since five are set daily and there are four solvers, these four divide 5 points each day. There are six *possible* divisions of these 5 points:

Division no.	1st solver	2nd solver	3rd solver	4th solver
1	5	0	0	0
2	4	1	0	0
3	3	2	0	0
4	3	1	1	0
5	2	2	1	0
6	2	1	1	1

(2) From the above can be calculated the amount of money which changes hands in respect of each division of points:

(1) Division no.	(2) Amounts in £ won or lost by				(3) Total amount changing hands
	1st solver	2nd solver	3rd solver	4th solver	
1	+ 15	− 5	− 5	− 5	15
2	+ 11	− 1	− 5	− 5	11
3	+ 7	+ 3	− 5	− 5	10
4	+ 7	− 1	− 1	− 5	7
5	+ 3	+ 3	− 1	− 5	6
6	+ 3	− 1	− 1	− 1	3

(3) Our objective is to construct from these data a "profit and loss" account for the five solvers, remembering (a) that each of them is a non-participant on one day out of the five; (b) that in order of successfulness A is never inferior to B, or B to C, and so on.

Here is the framework of our table:

Profit and Loss in £.

Setter:	A	B	C	D	E
A	—				
B		—			
C			—		
D				—	
E					—
Total	+ 20			− 12	− 12

(4) Now the only way in which a loss of £12 can be made up is by taking £5 twice and £1 twice; hence Division no. 6 must occur twice; this accounts for £6 out of £41. The balance of £35 can only be made up of one £15 and two £10 s; i.e. Division no. 3 occurs twice and Division no. 1 once.

(5) A never loses; his £20 is thus made up of two £7 s and

224

two £3 s. The remainder of the table now falls rapidly into place:

Profit and Loss in £.

Setter:	A	B	C	D	E
A	—	+ 15	− 5	− 5	− 5
B	+3	—	− 1	− 1	− 1
C	+3	− 1	—	− 1	− 1
D	+7	+ 3	− 5	—	− 5
E	+7	+ 3	− 5	− 5	—
Total	+ 20	+ 20	− 16	− 12	− 12

Thus B wins £20 on balance; C loses £16.

· 33 ·

CUBICLES

It is obvious that the "cubicles" derived from each cube will bear varying Totals, which cannot be less than 6 $(1 + 2 + 3)$ or more than 15 $(6 + 5 + 4)$. But the Totals of any particular set of cubicles will evidently depend upon the way in which its faces are numbered.

The six faces of a cube can be numbered (for the purposes of a problem of this type) in 15 different ways. For let the six faces be A, B, C, D, E and F. Then any one of the other five— say B—may be opposite to A. The remaining four form three pairs of opposites—C, D and E, F; C, E and D, F; C, F and D, E. Thus fifteen different sets of cubicles may be obtained from any one cube.

We can thus construct a table, showing for each possible set of cubicles the various Totals that will be obtained:

Opposite faces			Totals of:									
			6	7	8	9	10	11	12	13	14	15
65	43	21	.	.	.	1	3	3	1	.	.	.
65	42	31	.	.	1	1	2	2	1	1	.	.
65	41	32	.	.	1	2	1	1	2	1	.	.
64	53	21	.	.	1	1	2	2	2	1	.	.
64	52	31	.	1	.	2	1	1	2	.	1	.
64	51	32	.	1	1	1	1	1	1	1	1	.
63	54	21	.	.	1	2	1	1	2	1	.	.
63	52	41	1	.	.	3	.	.	3	.	.	1
63	51	42	1	.	1	1	1	1	1	1	.	1
62	54	31	.	1	1	1	1	1	1	1	1	.
62	53	41	1	.	1	1	1	1	1	1	.	1
62	51	43	1	1	.	.	2	2	.	.	1	1
61	54	32	.	1	2	1	.	.	1	2	1	.
61	53	42	1	.	2	.	1	1	.	2	.	1
61	52	43	1	1	.	1	1	1	1	.	1	1

(The above data are not all required for the present problem, but the reader may like to make use of them in the construction of other examples.)

There was *one* cubicle with a "Total" of fourteen in the Professor's hat. This can be deduced as follows:

(1) There were eleven cubicles in all with a total of nine. A cube can be divided so as to produce three cubicles with a Total of nine, but only in one way. This division produces no cubicle of fourteen or seven. The cube cannot be divided so as to produce more than three nine-total cubicles.

(2) Therefore three boys had divided their cube so as to produce three nine-totals, and one so as to produce two nine-totals.

(3) There is one way in which a cube can be divided so as to produce two nine-totals and Totals (one each) of seven and nine. The fourth boy had adopted this division, for his Total of seven was exhibited. *Hence there was one Total of fourteen in the hat.*

• 34 •

FOOTPRINTS IN THE SNOW

Richard, Vivian and Kitty have all hole-proof alibis. It follows that Clara is the murderess.

The crime had been planned by the four beneficiaries in concert.

Clara must have reached the bungalow soon after 4 p.m. (presumably in Vivian's car)—she left no footprints in the snow and Vivian was back at Chadbury at 4.30. She shot Miss Pennywise, we know, some time between 5.10 and 5.40. Presumably she was wearing gloves.

The 'phone call to her sister (who appears to have been an accessory) was to tell Vivian to be in readiness with the car.

Richard reached the bungalow at 6 p.m. and (according to plan) at once rang up the police. The snow, however, had made things awkward for Clara. Richard had no option but to carry her from the bungalow to Vivian's waiting car.

Here, at the last moment, there was some sort of quarrel; Richard was shot either by Vivian or by the indomitable Clara and a fake suicide arranged. Vivian had barely started up the car when they saw in the distance the lights of Inspector Guy's motor bicycle. He had just got Clara away in time.

• 35 •

CRACKRIB'S DIARY

Inspection of the table suggests that if there is a cipher it will be found in the last two figures of each "log". These are suspicious; for example, the digit 5 occurs at the end eleven times out of forty. This is contrary to all probability.

Comparison with a 7-figure table of logarithms confirms these suspicions. The "cipher" is to be found in the numbers:

20   15   84   51   25   etc.

Now of these numbers as many as 26 out of 40 are under 26. This at once suggests that 1, 2, 3, … 26 are being used as the letters of the alphabet, dummy figures being inserted before 1, 2, 3, … 9 to give some verisimilitude to the table.

It will at once be seen that the suggestion is well-founded. The entry, deciphered, reads:

"TO-DAY JUGGINS TOLD ME WHERE THEY STOWED THE SWAG".

• 36 •

TAKING A CHANCE

Arsen starts from two assumptions: that Burgler is distributing all his votes between Arsen and Crooke; and that Crooke is giving one vote to himself.

Thus the following distributions are possible:

		A.	B.	C.
Of Burgler's votes	{	3	–	– (1)
		2	–	1 (2)
		1	–	2 (3)
		–	–	3 (4)
Of Crooke's votes	{	2	–	1 (1)
		–	2	1 (2)
		1	1	1 (3)

Thus Arsen must consider 12 possibilities altogether, each of which may be taken as equally probable.
Setting these out in order, we can work out in each what distribution of Arsen's votes will give him the placing he desires.

Combination of B.'s and C.'s votes	Votes resulting for: A.	B.	C.	Distribution of A.'s votes which will give A. 2nd place A.	B.	C.
B. (1) and C. (1)	5	–	1	(None possible)		
,, ,, C. (2)	3	2	1	–	3	–
				–	2	1
				–	–	3
,, ,, C. (3)	4	1	1	(None possible; but he must vote: – 3 – or – – 3)		
B. (2) and C. (1)	4	–	2	–	–	3
,, ,, C. (2)	2	2	2	1	–	2
,, ,, C. (3)	3	1	2	–	1	2
				–	–	3
				–	3	–
B. (3) and C. (1)	3	–	3	–	–	3
				–	1	2
				–	2	1
				1	–	2
,, ,, C. (2)	1	2	3	2	–	1
,, ,, C. (3)	2	1	3	–	–	3
				1	–	2
				1	1	1
B. (4) and C. (1)	2	–	4	1	2	–
				1	1	1
				1	–	2
				–	1	2
				–	–	3
				2	–	1
,, ,, C. (2)	–	2	4	3	–	–
,, ,, C. (3)	1	1	4	2	1	–
				2	–	1
				1	–	2

Tabulating these possibilities:

Distribution of A.'s votes			No. of possibilities for which appropriate
A.	B.	C.	
3	–	–	1
2	1	–	1
2	–	1	3
1	2	–	1
1	–	2	5
1	1	1	2
–	2	1	2
–	1	2	3
–	3	–	3
–	–	3	7

Whence it is clear that Arsen's best chance is to give all three votes to Crooke.

• 37 •

THE SECOND BLOTTO PROBLEM

(1) Blotto must first consider (*a*) the possible distributions of his own forces, and (*b*) the distributions of the enemy forces appropriate in each case to a successful attack.

Distributions of the Blotto units			No. of possibilities	Best distribution of the attacking forces		
A	B	C	(Total $3^4 = 81$)	A	B	C
4	.	.	I	.	2	2
.	4	.	I	2	.	2
.	.	4	I	2	2	.
3	I	.	4	4	.	.
3	.	I	4	4	.	.
I	3	.	4	2	.	2
.	3	I	4	2	.	2
I	.	3	4	2	2	.
.	I	3	4	2	2	.
2	2	.	6	3	.	I
2	.	2	6	3	I	.
.	2	2	6	I	3	.
2	I	I	12	3	I	.
I	2	I	12	2	.	2
I	I	2	12	2	2	.

(2) From the above it is evident that the enemy

either must attack Fort A with 2 units and Fort B with 2 units;

or must attack Fort A with 2 units and Fort C with 2 units;

and that these attacking dispositions are equally probable.

(3) On the assumption that these attacking dispositions are equally probable, Blotto would distribute his forces in defence:

> 3 units in Fort A,
> 1 unit in Fort B.

No other distribution gives him so good an expectation of advantage.

(4) Hence the enemy commander, expecting the above defence, will launch all four units against Fort A; and therefore:

Blotto, to be certain of success, will place all his units in Forts B and C. The distribution of his forces as between these two forts is a matter of indifference.

• 38 •

NEVERLAND

(1) Let the distribution of the General's forces on July 1st be:

At Day:	x units
At Night:	y "
At Morrow:	z "

(2) Then as a result of the first order:

$\dfrac{x}{2}$ units are ordered to proceed to Night "to-morrow"

$\dfrac{x}{2}$ " " " Morrow "to-night"

$\dfrac{y}{2}$ " " " Day "to-morrow"

$\dfrac{y}{2}$ " " " Morrow "to-day"

$\dfrac{z}{2}$ " " " Day "to-night"

$\dfrac{z}{2}$ " " " Night "to-day"

(3) At 6 p.m. the distribution of forces is:

At Day:	x units,
At Night:	$\dfrac{y}{2} + \dfrac{z}{2}$ units,
At Morrow:	$\dfrac{y}{2} + \dfrac{z}{2}$ units.

(4) As a result of the second order:

$\dfrac{x}{4}$ units under orders to proceed to Night are ordered to remain at Day;

$\dfrac{x}{4}$ units under orders to proceed to Morrow are ordered to remain at Day;

$\dfrac{x}{4}$ units under orders to proceed to Day are ordered to remain at Morrow;

(5) Hence at midnight the distribution of forces is:

At Day: $\dfrac{3x}{4} + \dfrac{z}{4}$ units,

At Night: $\dfrac{y}{2} + \dfrac{z}{2}$ units,

At Morrow: $\dfrac{x}{4} + \dfrac{y}{2} + \dfrac{z}{4}$ units.

(6) As a result of the third order:

$\dfrac{z}{8}$ units are ordered to return from Day to Morrow

$\dfrac{z}{4}$ „ „ „ Night to „

(7) Hence at midnight on July 2nd the distribution is:

At Day: $\dfrac{x}{2} + \dfrac{y}{2} + \dfrac{z}{8}$ units.

At Night: $\dfrac{x}{4} + \dfrac{z}{4}$ units.

At Morrow: $\dfrac{x}{4} + \dfrac{y}{2} + \dfrac{5z}{8}$ units.

I.e.:
$$\dfrac{x}{2} + \dfrac{y}{2} + \dfrac{z}{8} = 26,$$
$$\dfrac{x}{4} + \dfrac{z}{4} = 24,$$
$$\dfrac{x}{4} + \dfrac{y}{2} + \dfrac{5z}{8} = 50,$$

Whence
$$x = 32,$$
$$y = 4,$$
$$z = 64.$$

At 8 a.m. on July 1st the General had 32 units at Day, 4 units at Night, and 64 units at Morrow.

• 39 •

THE 'PHLEGMATIC'S' RETURN VOYAGE

(1) The following table shows:

  (a) the partitions of six points among five competitors;

  (b) the amounts won or lost by each of five competitors, corresponding to these several partitions;

  (c) the corresponding amounts paid into the pool:

No.	Conundrums solved by					Winnings or losses in £ of					Total of pool
	1	2	3	4	5	1	2	3	4	5	
1	6	0	0	0	0	+ 24	− 6	− 6	− 6	− 6	£24
2	5	1	0	0	0	+ 19	− 1	− 6	− 6	− 6	£19
3	4	2	0	0	0	+ 14	+ 4	− 6	− 6	− 6	£18
4	4	1	1	0	0	+ 14	− 1	− 1	− 6	− 6	£14
5	3	3	0	0	0	+ 9	+ 9	− 6	− 6	− 6	£18
6	3	2	1	0	0	+ 9	+ 4	− 1	− 6	− 6	£13
7	3	1	1	1	0	+ 9	− 1	− 1	− 1	− 6	£ 9
8	2	2	2	0	0	+ 4	+ 4	+ 4	− 6	− 6	£12
9	2	2	1	1	0	+ 4	+ 4	− 1	− 1	− 6	£ 8
10	2	1	1	1	1	+ 4	− 1	− 1	− 1	− 1	£ 4

(2) In 6 days the pool totals £78. No two amounts paid in are the same. Hence the payments on the six days can only have been:

(1) £24, (2) £19, (3) £14, (4) £9, (5) £8, (6) £4

and the corresponding amounts payable to the most successful solver must have been:

(1) £24, (2) £19, (3) £14, (4) £9, (5) £4, (6) £4

(3) We can now construct as much as is required of our competition table:

Setters	Solvers					
	A	*B*	*C*	*D*	*E*	*F*
A		14	− 1	− 1	− 6	− 6
B	19		− 1	− 6	− 6	− 6
C	24	− 6		− 6	− 6	− 6
D ⎫	9	− 1	− 1			
E ⎬	4	4	− 1			
F ⎭	4	− 1	− 1			
Total	60	10	− 5	?	?	?

(*a*) A wins £60. He must therefore be the Setter under scheme (3) above.

(*b*) C loses the same amount each day. This can only be £1. Hence he must be the Setter under scheme (2).

The remainder of the relevant data are set out in the table above.

B on balance wins £10.

• 40 •
ALF'S LAST BID

Suspicion is aroused in the first instance by the fact that there is a Knave of Diamonds in each hand. This suggests that the Bridge hands are a "fake".

Next, consider the comment "There are 52 cards in the pack; this gives you a double chance". Double what? 52 = 2 x 26 (the number of letters in the alphabet).

To decipher the message, experiment will be necessary. Presumably, since "both hands are a bit muddled" each hand will prove to be an anagram. If we can find the words "Jess" or "Dublin" we shall be on the way to a solution.

Solvers will very soon hit on the clue.

The alphabet used is:

$$\spadesuit \text{ and } \diamondsuit \begin{cases} \text{A K Q J 10 9 8 7 6 5 4 3 2} \\ \text{A B C D E F G H I J K L M} \end{cases}$$

$$\heartsuit \text{ and } \clubsuit \begin{cases} \text{N O P Q R S T U V W X Y Z} \\ \text{A K Q J 10 9 8 7 6 5 4 3 2} \end{cases}$$

This gives for North's hand:

BEFJOSUDEFMPS

which resolves itself into:

JESS BUMPED OFF;

and for South's hand:

ADNTYABDILOTU

which becomes:

AT DUBLIN TO-DAY.

SOLUTIONS

1 C	2 L	3 U	4 N	5 G	6 U	7 N	8 F	9 O	10 R	11 D	12 E	13 D
14 L	O	R	A	L	15 S	I	R	R	O	16 O	N	E
17 A	18 F	I	R	E	19 U	S	E	R	20 M	O	R	N
21 Y	O	C	22 M	E	A	N	23 D	24 R	A	M	A	S
25 T	R	O	U	26 B	L	E	27 T	O	N	28 A	G	E
29 W	E	N	L	O	30 C	31 K	32 E	X	33 E	T	E	R
34 E	H	35 F	E	L	O	N	36 Q	U	A	R	R	37 I
38 N	E	T	39 T	L	E	40 I	U	41 M	42 O	A	43 R	S
44 T	A	R	R	45 E	D	46 G	O	L	D	C	U	P
47 Y	D	O	O	M	48 S	H	49 L	U	D	L	O	W

SALOPIAN
(The clues in italics, in the puzzle, refer to
A Shropshire Lad)

NOTES. *Across*: 14. Ref. to *beak*. 19. Anag. of *ruse*.
23. dr–amas. 42. Anag. of *soar*.
Down: 7. ensi(g)n *rev.* 9. orr(is). 27. te(em).
28. (Magna) Carta *rev.* 33. (b)ea(n).
35. Anag. of *fort*. 36. quid pro quo.
37. Anag. of *wisp*.

1 A	2 N	3 I	4 M	5 A	6 L	S	7 A	8 B	9 E	10 L	11 L	12 A
13 S	O	N	A	T	A	14 T	15 H	O	R	I	U	M
16 P	O	17 S	S	18 E	S	19 S	20 E	L	D	D	E	P
21 I	N	V	E	R	T	22 A	I	23 S	A	R	24 U	E
25 D	26 I	E	27 H	A	28 R	D	29 N	I	C	30 K	E	L
31 I	N	N	A	T	E	32 R	O	N	33 C	A	D	O
34 S	A	G	35 E	36 S	S	37 E	38 U	N	H	A	39 S	P
40 T	N	A	N	E	T	41 A	S	E	I	42 T	Y	S
43 R	E	L	I	V	44 E	S	45 E	R	E	H	N	I
46 A	R	I	S	E	S	47 E	U	S	F	E	F	S

SIXES AND SEVENS

NOTES. *Across*: 7. (Is)abella. 32. roncado(r). 47. Anag. of *effuses*.

   Down: 1. Anag. 3. In(es). 4. Anag. 8. bol(us).
   12. Anag. 24. deu (C.E.). 27. ha(bit).
   30. *Jungle Book*. 36. seve(n). 39. syn(tax).

1 S	2 O	3 V	4 E	R	5 E	6 I	7 G	8 N	9 T	E	10 A	11 K
12 A	M	I	C	13 A	B	L	E	14 A	R	15 E	N	A
16 P	N	E	U	M	A	17 T	I	C	18 O	R	A	L
19 R	I	20 N	D	21 A	22 S	H	23 S	E	24 G	A	G	E
25 O	S	I	E	R	26 K	A	T	27 E	28 L	29 O	R	N
P	30 C	A	R	D	I	N	31 A	L	32 O	D	A	D
33 H	I	T	34 L	35 E	36 R	37 A	U	K	38 D	I	M	S
39 Y	E	S	40 I	D	O	41 T	42 R	43 E	Y	44 E	45 N	46 A
47 T	N	B	A	I	S	O	A	W	48 T	R	O	P
49 E	T	A	R	R	E	S	50 M	E	E	R	U	T

MY DEAR WATSON

1 T	2 A	3 C	4 T	5 I	6 C	7 S	8 L	9 A	10 M	E	11 N	12 T
13 E	B	U	R	N	I	N	E	14 P	A	15 M	I	R
16 R	O	S	E	C	O	17 L	O	18 U	R	E	D	A
19 A	R	20 I	T	H	M	O	C	R	A	T	I	C
21 T	I	L	22 T	23 O	S	M	O	S	24 T	A	F	T
25 O	G	L	E	26 A	I	27 E	C	A	H	28 L	I	A
29 L	I	E	N	30 T	E	N	31 Y	32 N	O	33 R	C	R
34 O	N	35 G	R	I	S	T	36 T	I	N	E	37 A	I
38 G	A	39 A	I	V	40 S	41 T	I	G	42 M	A	T	A
43 Y	L	L	A	E	R	44 S	C	H	E	P	E	N

BELIEVE IT OR NOT

239

1 E	2 S	3 S	4 E	5 N	6 E	7 P	8 L	9 A	10 N	T	11 E	12 A
13 U	A	H	14 L	O	T	U	S	15 L	O	16 R	N	S
17 T	L	A	M	18 W	A	R	D	S	19 C	U	S	P
20 H	U	M	21 B	E	R	T	22 T	O	O	M	A	I
23 A	B	S	O	L	V	E	24 B	25 E	H	I	N	D
26 N	R	27 A	E	L	28 Y	N	I	M	O	N	G	I
29 A	I	R	30 R	31 O	T	A	32 R	U	R	33 A	U	S
34 S	O	U	35 N	D	I	N	G	36 U	T	T	I	T
37 I	U	M	38 O	R	C	39 C	H	O	S	E	N	R
40 A	S	C	R	I	B	E	41 S	Y	N	G	E	A

PER ARDUA AD ASPIDISTRA

1 M	2 E	3 R	4 I	5 D	6 I	7 O	8 N	9 A	10 L	I	11 T	12 Y
13 E	L	E	C	A	M	P	A	N	E	14 H	I	E
15 P	E	C	U	L	A	16 T	E	17 T	R	O	A	S
18 H	A	I	R	Y	19 M	A	B	20 I	R	O	N	T
21 I	N	P	22 O	23 U	R	I	24 N	G	25 I	D	26 L	E
27 S	28 T	R	29 A	N	G	L	E	30 O	U	31 T	E	R
32 T	R	O	P	E	33 S	O	O	N	34 Q	U	A	M
35 O	A	C	36 R	37 E	38 A	R	39 K	E	S	A	R	O
40 P	L	A	I	N	S	41 P	A	42 I	43 N	T	44 E	R
45 H	A	L	L	U	C	I	N	A	T	I	O	N

SWELL-FOOT'S DAUGHTER

NOTES.   *Across*: 13. A plant of the Aster family. 18. *The Hairy Ape* (O'Neill).   20. (Env)iron(s). 27. (Str)angle.   30. At Musketry. 33. (Bas)soon.   34. Quam(ash). 35. (R)oac(h). 45. Hall–ucination.

Down: 1,2. See derivation.   12. Both battles fought July 3rd. 16. Evan Harrington. 26. *King Lear*; Lear's *Nonsense Rhymes*. 28. *The Mikado*.   38. Now R.A.S.C. 42, 43. Anti(gone). 44. Eo(an).

1 L	2 E	3 X	4 I	C	5 O	6 G	7 R	8 A	9 P	10 H	I	11 C
12 E	B	U	L	13 L	I	E	N	C	E	14 E	15 N	O
16 V	O	L	T	17 I	N	N	18 A	T	E	L	Y	M
19 I	N	F	A	L	L	I	B	20 I	L	I	21 S	M
22 A	Y	23 E	24 A	Y	25 E	26 E	A	T	27 S	X	I	A
28 T	29 E	M	P	30 O	R	31 I	S	A	32 T	33 I	O	N
34 H	A	35 O	R	E	36 O	R	E	N	37 R	A	N	D
38 A	C	C	O	M	M	39 O	D	A	T	40 I	V	E
41 N	H	42 E	N	I	43 G	M	44 A	T	I	45 S	T	E
46 S	U	B	S	T	A	N	T	I	A	T	O	R

DERANGEMENT OF EPITAPHS

1 E	2 N	3 T	4 O	5 M	6 O	7 S	8 T	9 R	10 A	11 C	12 O	13 U	14 S
15 N	O	E	S	16 O	L	E	A	N	17 N	A	I	R	A
18 U	T	19 L	I	U	G	T	Y	R	20 A	I	R	21 A	U
22 M	A	P	23 E	S	24 A	U	25 T	26 O	27 C	R	A	N	E
28 E	B	U	29 Z	30 Q	31 U	T	O	32 L	O	O	S	33 I	R
34 R	I	T	A	35 U	R	I	M	36 E	L	37 P	E	A	K
38 A	L	N	39 P	E	N	T	A	40 D	41 U	L	42 R	43 U	R
44 T	I	45 I	O	46 T	47 R	48 S	T	E	T	49 A	P	T	A
O	50 T	U	T	51 A	E	52 N	O	T	H	I	53 M	I	U
54 R	E	Q	U	I	S	I	T	I	O	N	I	S	T

LOWER CRUSTACEAN

1 P	2 S	3 T	4 E	5 R	6 P	7 S	8 I	9 C	H	10 O	R	11 E
12 O	C	H	R	E	O	U	S	13 A	14 M	E	15 N	U
16 L	I	A	R	G	17 T	O	I	L	E	18 T	19 E	T
20 Y	A	L	21 L	A	22 O	N	S	L	A	U	23 A	E
24 H	M	I	25 A	I	M	26 E	27 D	I	28 G	H	T	R
29 Y	A	30 A	I	N	A	R	U	31 O	R	32 E	33 M	P
34 M	C	35 C	36 R	37 E	C	O	38 U	P	39 E	L	A	E
40 N	H	41 L	42 L	O	43 D	44 S	T	45 E	46 R	A	T	47 O
I	48 Y	I	D	D	I	49 S	H	50 L	A	T	I	N
51 A	M	O	S	52 M	E	L	P	O	M	E	N	E

MUSICAL CHAIRS

1 P	2 H	3 O	4 T	O	5 P	6 I	7 L	8 O	T	9 E	10 P	11 A
E	12 I	N	A	13 N	E	14 C	A	N	15 I	S	16 U	R
17 A	D	18 E	19 V	O	K	E	20 P	21 A	M	I	R	C
22 R	E	23 E	24 I	R	I	S	25 H	26 M	A	R	R	27 Y
28 S	29 E	R	A	30 S	N	31 O	O	P	32 M	A	33 C	E
34 P	R	O	N	E	35 R	E	E	L	S	36 S	R	A
L	37 A	D	D	38 L	E	39 S	R	E	40 T	E	41 A	S
42 U	S	43 E	44 N	E	M	Y	45 S	46 A	R	U	M	T
47 M	E	48 M	49 E	N	I	P	50 S	51 D	U	M	P	52 Y
53 E	M	U	S	54 A	T	T	I	C	55 E	S	A	E

FOR THE LITTLE ONES

1 A	2 S	3 S	A	S	4 S	5 I	6 T	7 E	8 R	9 M	10 I	11 C
12 S	O	13 A	14 B	15 D	T	A	O	16 L	A	U	G	H
17 S	O	R	L	I	A	18 S	T	I	19 R	S	20 N	R
21 I	N	D	I	G	22 C	O	23 E	M	A	24 T	O	Y
25 G	26 R	I	S	I	27 D	A	M	28 I	29 D	E	30 A	S
31 C	O	N	S	T	E	R	32 P	33 A	I	R	34 R	A
35 O	D	E	36 S	37 S	S	A	L	38 P	39 A	U	L	L
40 R	U	41 M	42 A	L	T	43 E	R	44 F	U	L	M	I
45 O	P	T	I	M	I	S	T	I	C	46 P	A	S

THE THIRTEEN NATIONS

1 P	R	2 O	3 S	4 P	5 E	6 R	7 O	8 A	9 W	10 F	11 U	12 L
13 O	14 G	15 T	R	I	N	C	U	L	O	16 E	V	E
17 R	O	18 B	19 E	S	20 M	21 E	T	A	L	22 R	A	G
23 N	N	24 R	C	A	25 I	W	W	26 S	27 E	D	28 N	A
29 O	Z	O	N	30 E	31 R	E	E	32 A	R	I	E	L
33 C	A	L	I	B	A	N	34 A	L	O	N	S	35 O
36 R	L	37 L	R	38 O	N	E	39 R	E	D	A	40 E	L
A	41 O	Y	P	N	42 D	C	43 Y	44 R	E	N	E	V
45 C	A	D	D	Y	46 A	K	I	N	E	47 D	N	A

SETEBOSH

1 P	2 H	I	3 L	A	4 N	5 T	6 H	R	7 O	8 P	9 I	10 C
11 E	A	12 R	L	13 Y	14 O	R	E	15 S	T	E	S	A
16 D	R	O	O	D	17 M	E	A	N	18 A	T	O	R
19 E	L	A	Y	20 A	I	21 R	T	I	G	22 H	23 T	A
24 S	E	N	D	25 E	N	A	26 S	27 P	O	O	R	C
28 T	Y	29 L	30 E	R	31 A	R	G	32 O	33 N	A	U	T
34 R	35 E	E	L	N	36 T	E	N	D	O	N	37 T	A
38 I	R	A	39 S	U	I	40 C	I	D	A	41 L	42 L	C
43 A	G	R	E	44 E	45 V	A	S	E	46 H	I	E	U
47 N	O	N	A	G	E	N	A	R	I	A	N	S

BIGOTRY AND VIRTUE

NOTES.   *Across*: 14. Anag. of *stereos*. 16. D–roo–d, Mystery of Edwin D. 18. a tor, rota. 28. Wat Tyler. 31. Argon–aut. 42. *loc. cit.* 43. ag–ree.

Down: 9. (b)iso(n). 12. (g)roan. 23. tru(mp), (h)urt. 29. l–earn. 35. Anag. of *gore*. 40. can(t).

1 P	**2** S	**3** Y	**4** C	**5** H	O	**6** A	**7** N	**8** A	L	**9** Y	**10** S	I	**11** S
A	**12** T	E	N	A	**13** C	I	O	U	**14** S	**15** A	C	**16** H	E
17 L	A	T	I	T	U	D	I	**18** N	A	R	I	A	N
19 I	L	**20** K	**21** D	E	I	**22** D	R	E	**23** A	E	O	N	S
24 M	I	N	E	R	**25** R	E	**26** S	T	R	**27** I	N	G	A
28 P	N	E	U	**29** M	**30** A	T	O	L	**31** O	G	**32** I	S	T
33 S	**34** P	E	C	I	M	E	N	**35** S	**36** P	O	R	**37** T	I
38 E	A	**39** S	E	**40** N	O	**41** L	**42** I	S	E	**43** R	K	O	O
44 S	T	E	R	I	**45** R	E	V	E	R	**46** S	**47** I	O	N
48 T	H	E	R	M	O	D	Y	N	A	M	I	C	S

WHEN WE WERE VERY JUNG

1 C	**2** P	A	N	**3** S	**4** I	**5** E	**6** S	**7** D	A	I	**9** S	**10** Y
11 O	A	**12** F	**13** P	E	R	T	U	R	B	**14** A	T	E
15 L	I	E	M	**16** R	I	C	E	**17** A	U	R	A	L
18 U	L	N	A	**19** I	S	H	**20** S	M	T	**21** M	I	L
22 M	**23** R	N	**24** R	O	**25** S	E	**26** M	A	**27** R	Y	**28** R	O
29 B	E	E	T	**30** U	N	S	E	T	**31** E	**32** M	**33** S	W
34 I	D	L	**35** E	S	**36** S	**37** L	N	I	L	I	O	B
38 N	A	**39** R	R	**40** O	W	L	Y	**41** C	**42** A	T	**43** E	O
44 E	R	U	**45** I	D	I	O	M	**46** J	E	R	R	Y
47 S	T	E	N	O	G	R	A	P	H	E	R	S

MINISTERING ANGEL

1 S	2 V	3 I	4 G	I	5 L	A	N	6 T	7 R	8 A	T	9 H
10 M	A	T	E	11 R	12 B	13 E	14 L	O	V	E	15 D	O
16 U	V	E	O	U	S	17 T	O	R	18 T	19 P	E	R
20 T	A	M	21 A	R	22 I	N	D	23 Q	U	I	E	T
24 T	S	25 A	R	I	N	A	26 E	U	R	E	27 K	A
28 I	O	N	29 I	T	C	30 H	31 S	E	N	32 R	A	T
33 N	U	T	S	34 A	U	N	T	35 M	36 A	R	D	I
37 E	R	I	E	38 N	R	U	39 O	A	T	40 O	I	O
41 S	42 A	C	43 R	I	S	T	44 N	D	45 E	T	46 O	N
47 S	I	S	S	A	48 O	S	E	A	49 B	S	O	S

THE MAY QUEEN

1 R	2 A	3 W	4 D	5 O	6 N	7 C	8 R	9 A	10 W	11 L	12 E	13 Y
A	14 M	A	I	N	15 E	L	E	P	H	A	N	T
16 R	E	B	E	C	C	A	S	H	A	R	17 P	I
18 E	R	E	19 M	E	T	I	E	R	20 T	K	A	C
21 W	I	22 L	23 L	24 I	A	M	D	O	25 B	26 B	I	27 N
28 A	C	I	D	29 A	R	30 M	31 A	32 I	R	33 O	R	I
34 G	35 E	O	36 R	G	37 E	O	38 S	B	O	R	39 N	E
40 R	M	41 N	O	O	K	42 R	E	43 I	L	D	E	L
44 A	M	E	45 L	46 I	A	S	E	D	L	E	Y	L
47 M	A	L	T	S	T	E	R	S	48 Y	L	N	O

VANITY FAIR

1 S	2 O	3 H	4 O	5 S	6 I	L	7 T	8 E	D	9 R	10 U	11 E
12 H	E	A	V	E	N	13 K	I	S	14 S	I	N	G
15 A	R	T	16 A	L	D	O	17 O	18 P	U	S	19 P	O
20 M	21 A	C	T	U	I	22 N	N	R	23 P	24 E	R	25 A
26 S	C	H	E	27 G	R	I	S	I	28 S	T	E	T
29 P	A	M	30 D	31 I	E	G	32 L	33 M	A	U	V	E
34 O	35 N	E	36 A	R	C	37 H	E	R	Y	38 T	A	39 O
40 N	I	N	N	41 Y	42 A	I	T	43 O	44 I	S	I	N
45 G	A	T	L	46 A	R	C	H	47 S	N	A	L	C
E	48 P	L	U	M	T	R	E	E	G	U	M	E

PRINCE OF DENMARK

NOTES. *Across*: 16. Aldo(us). 19. po(et). 20. Anag. of Actium. 22. nnr = inner–i.e. 23. Anag. of *pear*. 26. sche(me). 29. map *rev*. 30. glide. 43. (v)oisin.

Down: 1. Sham(rock). 9, 8. *The Sun Also Rises*. 14. sup(pose). 21. A.C.A. 24. Anag. of *statue*. 37. Anag. of *rich*. 39. Anag. of *cone*. 42. (H)art(y).

1 T	2 O	3 R	4 T	5 M	6 E	7 D	8 I	9 S	10 M	11 I	12 T	H
13 T	S	I	14 O	15 I	S	E	16 G	17 R	I	D	18 O	19 R
20 A	L	21 A	22 R	C	S	23 I	24 R	O	N	25 A	26 C	E
T	27 O	28 D	E	O	29 E	30 T	A	C	31 E	32 P	I	G
33 E	34 R	E	A	35 N	36 O	O	M	37 K	38 C	O	D	I
39 M	A	C	40 M	41 A	T	E	42 S	43 M	H	T	44 E	45 N
46 A	T	47 I	48 S	R	E	49 S	50 T	O	A	51 A	52 D	O
N	53 E	54 V	E	N	55 V	56 A	U	D	57 R	58 A	L	S
59 I	60 N	C	61 A	62 O	V	E	63 R	64 E	C	N	O	E
65 S	O	S	66 S	H	A	M	67 F	O	L	D	68 C	E

SPLITS

NOTES. *Across*: 1, 14. Test U do. 18. (F)or(d). 20. Al (Capone). 27. (R)odeo. 33. (c)erea(l). 42. th(e)m(e)s. 47. rise. 51. muoch = much about nothing. 53. Even(lode). 55. vaud(eville). 59. G.B. Shaw. 63. once (upon a time).

Down: 6. (W)esse(x). 8. (w)ig. 11. adi(pose). 38. char(lady). 60, 62. Nova Scotia. 64. cl(ear).

249

1 C	2 H	3 A	4 R	5 L	6 E	7 S	8 S	9 T	U	10 A	11 R	12 T
13 A	E	R	O	14 A	R	I	C	E	15 E	R	A	H
16 P	A	T	T	E	R	17 E	E	L	S	18 C	T	O
19 A	V	I	A	T	O	R	20 N	G	U	21 S	T	M
22 B	E	S	T	23 U	N	R	E	A	L	24 R	Y	A
25 L	26 A	T	E	R	27 E	A	S	E	L	E	28 S	S
29 A	R	I	S	T	O	30 T	31 E	32 L	I	A	N	M
33 N	I	C	34 E	35 I	U	O	36 T	E	37 A	38 L	O	O
39 C	E	40 L	T	41 C	S	A	R	42 E	L	M	E	R
43 A	L	E	X	A	N	D	E	R	P	O	P	E

BIOGRAPHY AND BOTANY

NOTES.   *Across*: 14. Erica.   17. less.   18. O.T.C.   20 gun;
gnu.   25. l–ate–r.   27. (c)easeless.
29. Fanny's First Play.   35. I.O.U.
38. Waterloo.   39. "The Celtic Fringe."
41. R.A.S.C.

Down: 2. he–ave.   5. teal (duck).   11. *The Wind
in the Willows*.   12. witho-*ut opia*-tes.
23. urtica = the stinging nettle.   28. peons
= pawns.   37. "*Happy is England*."

¹T	²P	³O	L	⁴L	⁵U	⁶X	⁷H	⁸A	⁹N	¹⁰S	¹¹I	¹²T
¹³W	A	L	¹⁴R	U	S	¹⁵O	E	M	O	¹⁶W	O	W
¹⁷E	R	I	E	¹⁸P	¹⁹U	S	S	Y	C	A	T	E
²⁰E	C	²¹I	T	²²O	N	²³A	I	R	²⁴A	L	A	E
D	²⁵H	E	N	G	I	S	T	²⁶C	A	L	²⁷U	D
²⁸L	E	D	E	²⁹A	V	L	A	³⁰A	³¹H	³²O	W	L
E	³³D	³⁴I	P	³⁵G	A	I	T	³⁶S	O	W	³⁷L	E
³⁸D	³⁹O	O	R	⁴⁰I	L	⁴¹A	I	⁴²T	R	I	A	D
U	⁴³S	W	A	N	⁴⁴V	⁴⁵O	O	⁴⁶O	S	N	O	E
⁴⁷M	L	A	C	⁴⁸T	E	R	N	⁴⁹R	A	G	D	E

TWO BY TWO

NOTES.　　*Across*: 7. Hans Andersen.　15. (R)omeo.
　　　　　　　20. not-ice.　33. dip(tera).　44. voodoo.
　　　　　　　46. noose.
　　　　Down: 3. (s)oli(d).　8. Mary.　9. (I)con.　24. A.A.
　　　　　　　27. "Mr Wu."　37. load.　39. Osl(o).

251

1 E	2 P	3 I	4 S	5 C	6 O	7 P	8 A	9 L	10 I	11 A	12 N	13 S
14 U	N	R	E	A	L	I	T	Y	15 B	R	I	O
16 C	E	R	E	B	R	O	S	17 P	I	N	A	L
A	18 U	I	T	L	A	N	19 D	E	20 R	21 O	R	E
22 L	M	S	23 H	E	24 C	E	I	L	I	25 N	G	C
Y	26 A	I	E	R	27 Y	28 E	F	F	E	N	29 D	I
30 P	T	O	31 S	32 C	A	R	F	33 A	N	I	A	S
34 T	I	N	H	A	T	35 D	E	F	36 I	37 C	I	T
U	38 C	39 H	E	S	S	40 C	R	I	N	O	L	I
41 S	T	A	P	H	Y	L	O	M	A	T	I	C

ET EGO IN ARCADIA

NOTES. *Across*: 15. Con brio. 16. Cerebro-spinal meningitis = spotted fever. 22. Sir Josiah Stamp is President of the L.M.S. 23. He-man. 26. Aiery = Aerie. 33. (An)anias. 34. Tin Hat = staff officer. 40. Crinoli(ne).

Down: 6. Don Carlo(s). 8,9. Salty. 11. Florence. 31. Shep(herd). 32. C–ash; Omar Khayyam. 33. Faim. 36. (Pat)ina. 37. Three meanings.

1 P	2 A	3 N	D	O	4 R	5 A	6 T	7 H	E	8 S	I	9 S
10 Y	R	O	11 T	12 A	P	I	13 C	I	14 T	N	15 A	A
16 T	I	D	A	L	17 A	N	A	18 T	R	O	U	T
19 H	E	U	R	I	S	T	I	20 C	21 O	I	L	U
22 A	L	L	E	G	E	23 L	R	I	W	T	E	R
24 G	25 A	E	S	26 H	E	E	27 O	D	28 E	R	29 S	N
30 O	R	31 E	32 S	T	E	S	33 B	34 O	L	35 E	36 R	A
37 R	E	G	A	38 L	39 I	A	40 O	A	T	S	41 A	L
42 A	N	A	L	Y	S	E	S	43 R	E	N	N	I
44 S	A	L	E	S	M	A	N	S	H	I	P	A

AGAIN THE RINGER

DOUBLE ACROSTICS

SOLUTIONS

• 1 •
HANDSAW
OKLAHOMA
L   O   T
M I D A S
E R A T O
S A T A N

• 2 •
G R U B
O M E G A
L A B E L
F A L L

• 3 •
LOTHARIO
A   M   P   ERE
E A C H
R A T T L E
T A E L
E   L   I
S A M O A

• 4 •
C U C K OO
H E N R I
A R I A N
R   A   G   OUT
L A U R A
E   O   N
S W O R D
S O P H I S M
T A R A R A
ST U T T E R
A R T I S T
R OYALTY
T U P P E R

• 5 •
E L E P H A N T
U K E L E L E
C   O   W
L A N C E L O T
I   D   O
D A R I E N

• 6 •
S P I N A C H
P L A N E
A T A R A X I A
D O C T O R
E L I O T
S N A R K S

• 7 •

```
S O R I T E S
A R E T H U S A
I     B     I S
N   E   O N
T   O   R T
G E O R G I A
E R E W H O N
O   R E A D
R O A D M E N D E R
E     D     W IN
```

• 8 •

```
B O M B
U B I Q U E
L O R N A
L U N A R
```

• 9 •

```
  C E N S U S
  H A M L E T
Z E P P E L I N
  D A I L
  D I E T
  A L T O
  R O M A N
```

• 10 •

```
G R O U S E
E N O W
E U R E K A
S O L O N
E U R I P I D E S
```

• 11 •

```
H E R O D
U R D U
MEERSCHAUM
P U M P
T H I B E T
Y E S T E R D A Y
```

• 12 •

```
V I C T O R I A
I     R     E  LAND
R O D I N
G R A C E
I C E N I
L   O   N   D  ON
```

• 13 •

```
B   E   A   K
I M O G E N
SALMAGUNDI
H E M I N G  WAY
O B A D I A H
PALIMPSEST
```

• 14 •

```
     ONOMATOPOEIC
ATA X    I    A
     F A S C I S M
     O L A F F U B
     R   O   V   E   R
     D   A   I   L   I
     A L M O N D
     N O T H I N G
     D   O   G   E
```

• 15 •

```
E   N   I   D
P I N E R O
S W A L L O W
O R I O N
MENELAUS
```

• 16 •

```
A   R   A   B
U S H E R
S   O   H   O
TALISMAN
EVEREST
NEVERMORE
```

ACROSTAGRAMS

• 1 •

```
L Y R I C
U L C E R
S C O U T
R O M E
E   E   L
```

• 2 •

```
T U R N I P
ANEMONE
P U M A
E   M   I   T
```

Note. Light: (4) "Time"
reversed.

• 3 •

```
T   U   B
A N V I L
B O R E
L A U R A
E A S T
```

• 4 •

```
H E R O D
A G A P E
T   E   A
EVEREST
DEARTH
```

Notes. (2) A–gape.
(5) Dearth—anagram of
thread

• 5 •

```
P R I A M
O R I N O C O
E     M     P     IRE
M E L P O M E N E
```

• 6 •

```
M A R I N E R
A S P I D I S T R A
R     O     O     M
B     O M     B
L A B I A L
E     V     E
```

• 7 •

```
P U M P
L O N E
E N D E D
A G E N D A
D E V I L
```

• 8 •

```
L A G E R
U K E L E L E
S T A R S
T I T I P U
R E G A L
E V E R E S T
```
Note. (1) Regal = Lager reversed.

• 9 •

```
M E A T
A L C O V E
T I T A N I A
E   R A M
```
Notes. (2) contains "Cove".
(4) Mare reversed.

• 10 •

```
M O R A L
D I   G I T
L O O M
E V E
S A N D S
```
Notes. Upright: (1) Miles = Latin for "soldier".
Lights: (3) Loom: Two meanings.
(5) Sands: "The Sands of Dee".

257

• 11 •

T A R
ENIGMA
ARARAT
R A C E

• 12 •

R O M E
INNER
C A P R I CORN
ERRATIC

Notes. (1) "Eric, or Little by Little."
(2) *Inner*, in musketry.

• 13 •

SAHARA
E E L
ANTIQUE
L A K E S

• 14 •

M O O R
OPORTO
R E A L M
E W E

Notes. Lights: (1) Othello, the Moor of Venice.
(3) D.O.R.A.
(4) Ewe = you.

ANAGRAMS

SOLUTIONS

• 1 •
Five Ordinary Words
1. INDEFEASIBLE
2. REVERBERATED
3. TOTEMISTIC
4. PREDESTINATION
5. INCALCULABILITY

• 2 •
Five More Ordinary Words
1. PALIMPSEST
2. ICONOCLAST
3. CONTINENTAL
4. CORROBORATION
5. PREOCCUPATION

• 3 •
Five Ordinary Words
1. CELANDINE
2. MEDICINAL
3. DISCLAIMER
4. CLANDESTINE
5. CANDLESTICK

• 4 •
Five Famous Novels
1. VANITY FAIR
2. PRIDE AND PREJUDICE
3. DOMBEY AND SON
4. GUY MANNERING
5. THE VICAR OF WAKEFIELD

• 5 •
Five Heroes of Antiquity
1. THEMISTOCLES
2. ALEXANDER
3. MILTIADES
4. JULIUS CAESAR
5. HORATIUS COCLES

• 6 •
Five English Plays
1. SHE STOOPS TO CONQUER
2. MAN AND SUPERMAN
3. THE SCHOOL FOR SCANDAL
4. THE WAY OF THE WORLD
5. EVERY MAN IN HIS HUMOUR

• 7 •
Five Modern Novels
1. ANN VERONICA
2. FAREWELL TO ARMS
3. THE FORSYTE SAGA
4. SINISTER STREET
5. GREEN APPLE HARVEST

• 8 •
Five Ordinary Words
1. DECREPIT
2. PREDICAMENT
3. REDUPLICATE
4. REPRODUCTIVE
5. UNPRECEDENTED

DUOGRAMS

SOLUTIONS

• 9 •
European towns

1. MOSCOW—BERNE
2. BERLIN—VIENNA
3. MADRID—AMSTERDAM
4. HAMBURGH—MARSEILLES
5. CONSTANTINOPLE—TURIN

• 11 •
American Cities

1. NEW YORK—BOSTON
2. SAN FRANCISCO—DETROIT
3. WASHINGTON—CHICAGO
4. MINNEAPOLIS—DULUTH
5. CINCINNATI—NEW ORLEANS

• 10 •
English Towns

1. LONDON—MANCHESTER
2. YORK—BIRMINGHAM
3. SOUTHAMPTON—LEEDS
4. NORWICH—LEICESTER
5. BRISTOL—PETERBOROUGH

• 12 •
Wild Animals

1. SLOTH—GIRAFFE
2. ARMADILLO—TIGER
3. CAMEL—ELEPHANT
4. RHINOCEROS—HIPPOPOTA-
   MUS
5. DROMEDARY—LEOPARD

MISCELLANEOUS

SOLUTIONS

(1) REVEL—LEVER

(2) KATE'S—TEAKS—STEAK—KEATS—SKATE—TAKES—STAKE

(3) EROS—SORE

(4) CLOUT

LOUT

OUT

(5) NEMO—OMEN

(6)

L	A	I	R
O	G	R	E
G	R	I	N
E	A	S	T

(7)

P	O	R	E
A	M	E	N
L	E	N	O
S	N	O	W

(8) LAGER—REGAL

(9) STRING
TRING
RING

(10) PLEASE
LEASE
EASE

(11) ROMA—AMOR

(12) WARDER reversed and bisected
= RED and RAW.

(13) SHARK
HARK
ARK

(14) WHEELS
HEELS
EELS

(15) REBUT—TUBER

(16) STRAIN
TRAIN
RAIN

(17) CLEAR
LEAR
EAR

PALINDROMIC WORD-SQUARES

SOLUTIONS

(1) "Lived irate Val, a vet., a rid-evil."
L I V E D
I R A T E
V A L A V
E T A R I
D E V I L

(2) "Revel ever. Even Eve, revel ever."

```
R E V E L
E V E R E
V E N E V
E R E V E
L E V E R
```

(3) "Pater arose to note so rare tap."

```
P A T E R
A R O S E
T O N O T
E S O R A
R E T A P
```

(4) "Lived I, mad Eva, saved amid evil."

```
L I V E D
I M A D E
V A S A V
E D A M I
D E V I L
```

(5) "Dora tones area; erase not a rod."

```
D O R A T
O N E S A
R E A E R
A S E N O
T A R O D
```

CARD PROBLEMS

BIDDING PROBLEMS AT CONTRACT BRIDGE

SOLUTIONS

• 1 •

North should bid Three Diamonds

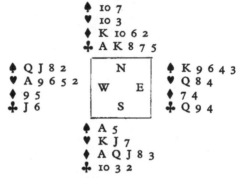

Score: Love-all. South deals

The bidding:

South	1 ♦	5 ♦
West	No Bid	No Bid
North	3 ♦	No Bid
East	No Bid	No Bid

After South's bid of One Diamond, North has a double raise, based on the following calculation of supporting tricks:

♠ 10 7	1 (for the doubleton with 4 trumps)
♥ 10 3	
♦ K 10 6 2	½ (for the K)
	½ (for a fourth trump)
♣ A K 8 7 5	2 (for the A K)
	1 (for the 2 "long" tricks)
Total	5 Supporting tricks

N.B.—This "jump" raise in the bid suit is *not* forcing.

264

South has a double re-bid. His hand is worth 5 ½ playing tricks, which, as he is not vulnerable, justifies the try for game.

The contract will only be defeated if South loses his Ace of Spades before he has established Dummy's Clubs. If South bid Three No Trump (on the assumption that North controlled Clubs) he would have the same difficulty to contend with.

· 2 ·

South should make No Bid

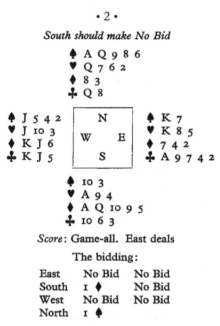

♠ A Q 9 8 6
♥ Q 7 6 2
♦ 8 3
♣ Q 8

♠ J 5 4 2   ♠ K 7
♥ J 10 3   ♥ K 8 5
♦ K J 6   ♦ 7 4 2
♣ K J 5   ♣ A 9 7 4 2

♠ 10 3
♥ A 9 4
♦ A Q 10 9 5
♣ 10 6 3

Score: Game-all. East deals

The bidding:

East	No Bid	No Bid
South	1 ♦	No Bid
West	No Bid	No Bid
North	1 ♠	

A "biddable" suit (especially if a major) should be shown by the supporting hand on about 1 ½ honour-tricks. This is a "semi-forcing" bid; it invites the original declarer to continue if he has anything at all to show. This is the "One over One" principle, at present coming much into favour among experts, for which Mr Theodore Lightner is primarily responsible.

In the present case the bidding ends with North's One Spade. South has a bare minimum bid. To respond even with One No Trump (which South would almost certainly fail to make) would be very misleading.

In play, North will have hard work to make his contract. The distribution of his adversaries' cards is exceptionally unfavourable.

West, if not vulnerable, could have overcalled South's Diamond bid with One No Trump. Here again the play of the hand would be full of interest.

• 3 •

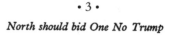

North should bid One No Trump

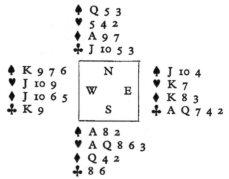

```
                    ♠ Q 5 3
                    ♥ 5 4 2
                    ♦ A 9 7
                    ♣ J 10 5 3
   ♠ K 9 7 6          N           ♠ J 10 4
   ♥ J 10 9                       ♥ K 7
   ♦ J 10 6 5      W     E        ♦ K 8 3
   ♣ K 9             S            ♣ A Q 7 4 2
                    ♠ A 8 2
                    ♥ A Q 8 6 3
                    ♦ Q 4 2
                    ♣ 8 6
```

Score: E—W, game; N—S, love. South deals

The bidding:

South	1 ♥	No Bid
West	No Bid	No Bid
North	1 N T	
East	No Bid	

The "negative" Take-out of One No Trump, over an opening Suit-bid of One, is one of the leading features of the Forcing System. Its object is to keep the bidding alive—in case partner has opened on a hand containing 3 or more honour-tricks—while showing that one's own strength is strictly limited.

The One No Trump bid shows *about 1 ½ honour-tricks, distributed between two or more suits;* but its negative implications are not less important. These are:

(1) Not more than 2 to 2 ½ honour-tricks (as in that case, in the absence of a biddable suit, the raise would be Two No Trump).

(2) No biddable suit (as a suit should always be shown if possible).

(3) Inadequate trump support for partner.

North's hand, in our example, precisely conforms to these conditions.

South cannot re-bid, as he has nothing to show beyond his initial declaration. A bid of Two Hearts would suggest undisclosed strength.

If East were not vulnerable he might attempt a bid of Two Clubs. But nothing is gained by risking a bid, when vulnerable, after West has already passed.

The probability is that North will just make his contract.

• 4 •

North should bid Three No Trump

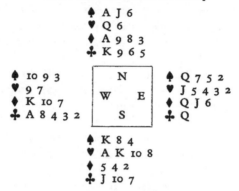

♠ A J 6
♥ Q 6
♦ A 9 8 3
♣ K 9 6 5

♠ 10 9 3   ♠ Q 7 5 2
♥ 9 7   ♥ J 5 4 3 2
♦ K 10 7   ♦ Q J 6
♣ A 8 4 3 2   ♣ Q

          N
     W   E
          S

♠ K 8 4
♥ A K 10 8
♦ 5 4 2
♣ J 10 7

Score: Love-all. South deals

The bidding:

South	1 ♥	No Bid
West	No Bid	No Bid
North	3 N T	
East	No Bid	

South, being not vulnerable, has a straightforward opening One Heart bid. West might, as a deterrent to North, attempt a bid of Two Clubs; but on the whole I think his hand too weak. North, with 3 honour-tricks and fair intermediate cards, should go boldly for game in No Trump; he cannot attempt a Forcing Take-out as he has no biddable suit. North's bid of course "buys" the contract.

East's opening lead is difficult. If he leads a small Spade, which is probably best, North should have no difficulty with his contract.

• 5 •

North should bid Four No Trump

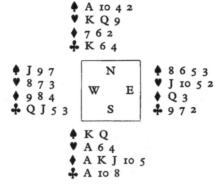

♠ A 10 4 2
♥ K Q 9
♦ 7 6 2
♣ K 6 4

♠ J 9 7   ♠ 8 6 5 3
♥ 8 7 3   ♥ J 10 5 2
♦ 9 8 4   ♦ Q 3
♣ Q J 5 3   ♣ 9 7 2

♠ K Q
♥ A 6 4
♦ A K J 10 5
♣ A 10 8

Score: Game-all. West deals

The bidding:

West	No Bid	No Bid	No Bid
North	No Bid	4 N T	No Bid
East	No Bid	No Bid	No Bid
South	2 ♦	6 N T	

North, being vulnerable, has not an original bid (not vulnerable, however, he would have a perfectly good One No Trump). Thanks to his initial pass, South can read his hand on the second round with precision. There must be at least 2 ½ honour-tricks; there cannot be more; and the combinations of honours available for North are very limited.

South's contract of Six No Trump is therefore a virtual certainty. Grand Slam, however, should not be attempted as the situation of the ♦ Q is unknown; or, alternatively, it is just possible that the adversaries hold the ♠ A.

• 6 •

East should bid Five Diamonds

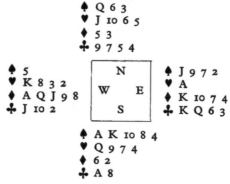

♠ Q 6 3
♥ J 10 6 5
♦ 5 3
♣ 9 7 5 4

♠ 5   N   ♠ J 9 7 2
♥ K 8 3 2   ♥ A
♦ A Q J 9 8   W   E   ♦ K 10 7 4
♣ J 10 2   ♣ K Q 6 3
              S

♠ A K 10 8 4
♥ Q 9 7 4
♦ 6 2
♣ A 8

Score: **Game-all. South deals**

The bidding:

South	1 ♠	No Bid
West	2 ♦	No Bid
North	No Bid	No Bid
East	5 ♦	

For a two-trick overcall, vulnerable, defending hand needs about 2 honour-tricks, a good five-card suit, and four fairly certain trump tricks. West's hand just fulfils these conditions.

East, with 3 honour-tricks and about 6 supporting tricks, can make a direct bid for game. West should not raise again. There is nothing in his hand not implied in his original bid.

In play, West will take his eleven tricks.

• 7 •

East should make No Bid

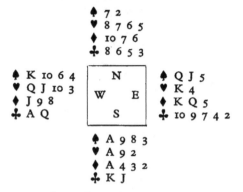

Score: Game-all. South deals

The bidding:

South	1 N T	No Bid
West	Double	
North	No Bid	
East	No Bid	

Here is an example of the "business" pass. South, with 3 ½ honour-tricks, cannot but bid One No Trump; but North has a complete "bust". West's is a daring double, but justified by his high "intermediates".

East passes, since on his hand a heavy penalty is certain. South is trapped without means of escape. Whatever West leads (barring, of course, a Club), South can only make his three Aces—a penalty of 1400 points.

Actually, West will lead the Queen of Hearts.

• 8 •

South should Double

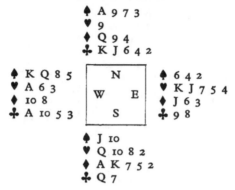

♠ A 9 7 3
♥ 9
♦ Q 9 4
♣ K J 6 4 2

♠ K Q 8 5 ♠ 6 4 2
♥ A 6 3 ♥ K J 7 5 4
♦ 10 8 ♦ J 6 3
♣ A 10 5 3 ♣ 9 8

♠ J 10
♥ Q 10 8 2
♦ A K 7 5 2
♣ Q 7

Score: Game-all. East deals

The bidding:

East	No Bid	1 ♥	No Bid	No Bid
South	1 ♦	Double	2 N T	No Bid
West	Double	No Bid	No Bid	No Bid
North	Re-double	2 ♣	3 N T	

The exchange of inferences here made possible is well worth studying. North, by his re-double, shows 2+ honour-tricks; East calls attention to his Heart suit; South, by doubling East's bid, asks North for further information. North now shows his best suit, the Clubs, and South displays his stoppers in Hearts. North, arguing that South would not bid Two No Trump, in the face of the Honour tricks to the left of him, without a double guard in Hearts, can now reasonably take a chance on Three No Trump. The contract can be made against any defence.

AUCTION AND CONTRACT BRIDGE

*Problems of Bidding, illustrated by actual hands from
the Culbertson-Lenz match.*

SOLUTIONS
[analysis by Ely Culbertson]

The Contract bidding is given as it actually occurred. The
Auction bidding is that which Mr Culbertson recommends.

• 9 •

**TAKE-OUT DOUBLE, WITH A
GOOD BIDDABLE SUIT**

Auction Bidding

South	West	North	East
		Pass	Pass
I N T	Double	2 ♣	Pass
Pass	2 ♠	Pass	Pass
Pass			

Contract Bidding

South	West	North	East
		Pass	Pass
I ♦	Double[1]	2 ♣	Pass[2]
Pass	2 ♠[3]	Pass	Pass
3 ♣[4]	3 ♠[5]	Pass	4 ♠[6]
Pass	Pass	Pass	

Contract: 4 ♠ by Mr Culbertson.
Result: Made five.
Lead: ♣ J by Mr Lenz.

ANALYSIS OF CONTRACT BIDDING

[1] The hand contains 3 ½ honour-tricks plus a Queen and is prepared for either a Heart or Spade response. If partner should bid
Clubs, the long Spade suit offers a safe refuge.

[2] Mrs Culbertson's hand is too weak for a free response.

[3] I now show my strong, biddable Spade suit.

[4] An unwise re-opening of the bidding.

[5] The playing-trick strength justifies a re-bid.

[6] In view of the Take-out Double and my two bids, Mrs Culbertson's hand is strong enough, with the Heart King and adequate trump support, for a Raise.

• 10 •

A FORCING TAKE-OUT

Auction Bidding

South	West	North	East
			1 N T
Pass	2 ♥	Pass	Pass
Pass			

Contract Bidding

South	West	North	East
			1 N T[1]
Pass	3 ♥[2]	Pass	4 ♥[3]
Pass	Pass	Pass	

Contract: 4 ♥ by Mr Culbertson.
Result: Made four.
Lead: ♠ 10 by Mr Lenz.

ANALYSIS OF CONTRACT BIDDING

[1] The hand contains 3½ honour-tricks and no biddable suit. It is thus a sound Opening bid of One No Trump vulnerable.

[2] I hold 3 honour-tricks and a two-suited hand; plenty of strength to assure a game after partner's Opening bid.

[3] With adequate trump support, the Raise to game in Hearts is much safer than to try for game at Three No Trump, even with the evenly distributed hand.

• 11 •

A SLAM FOLLOWING A FORCING TAKE-OUT

Auction Bidding

South	West	North	East
			1 ♥
Pass	1 ♠	Pass	Pass
Pass			

Contract Bidding

South	West	North	East
			1 ♥¹
Pass	2 ♠²	Pass	3 ♠³
Pass	6 ♠⁴	Pass	Pass
Pass			

Contract: 6 ♠ by Mr Culbertson.
Result: Made six.
Lead: ♦ 10 by Mr Lenz.

ANALYSIS OF CONTRACT BIDDING

[1] The Heart suit is not quite strong enough to bid ordinarily. However, it is better to bid a shaded suit when vulnerable than to open the bidding with One No Trump.

[2] This bid, a Jump of more than necessary to overcall after partner has opened the bidding, is known as a Forcing Take-out. Neither partner may drop the bidding until a game contract has been reached. A Forcing Take-out may be made on something more than 3 honour-tricks. My hand contains 5 honour-tricks and it is only necessary to find favourable distribution to justify a Slam bid.

[3] Disclosing adequate support for partner's Forcing Take-out.

[4] My partner's Opening bid and Raise of the Spade suit has shown a hand containing more than 2 ½ honour-tricks, as well as support for the trump suit I bid. With my holding of 5 honour-tricks and about 3 indicated in Mrs Culbertson's hand, the Slam bid is sound.

· 12 ·

PREFERRING GAME TO PENALTY

Auction Bidding

South	West	North	East
	1 ♥	1 ♠	4 ♥
4 ♠	Double	Pass	5 ♥
Pass	Pass	Pass	

Contract Bidding

South	West	North	East
	1 ♥	1 ♠	4 ♥[1]
4 ♠[2]	Double[3]	Pass	5 ♥[4]
Pass	Pass	Pass	

Contract: 5 ♥ by Mr Culbertson.
Result: Made five.
Lead: ♠ 3 by Mr Lenz.

ANALYSIS OF CONTRACT BIDDING

[1] The hand has sufficient playing-tricks to justify an immediate Raise to game. No good purpose would be served by Mrs Culbertson showing her Diamonds.

[2] While South's hand is weak in honour-tricks, it is fairly strong distributionally and our opponents were not vulnerable.

[3] Offering partner a choice between playing to defeat opponents or to raise the Heart contract. The Penalty Double does not preclude my partner from continuing the bidding if the distribution suggests that it is likely to produce the better result.

[4] Wisely preferring the game. As a matter of fact, the distribution is such that Four Spades could be made.

· 13 ·

FINAL NO TRUMP RESPONSE TO
OPENING SUIT-BID

Auction Bidding

South	West	North	East
	Pass	Pass	1 ♥
Pass	2 ♦	Pass	2 N T
Pass	Pass	Pass	

Contract Bidding

South	West	North	East
	Pass	Pass	1 ♥[1]
Pass	2 ♦[2]	Pass	2 N T[3]
Pass	2 ♦[4]	Pass	3 N T[5]
Pass	Pass	Pass	

Contract: 3 No Trump by Mrs Culbertson.
Result: Made three.
Lead: ♥ Q by Mr Jacoby.

ANALYSIS OF CONTRACT BIDDING

[1] Mrs Culbertson's hand contains 3 ½ honour-tricks and a biddable suit. The correct Opening bid is One Heart.

[2] Although I hold only 1 plus honour-trick, the absence of Hearts and the length of the suit require a Two Diamond response.

[3] Disclosing re-bid strength in the hand, but not in the suit.

[4] Showing the re-bid strength of the suit.

[5] With all suits stopped, the No Trump contract appears the best for the combined hands. Game at Diamonds could be made due to the location of the Club honours, but game at No Trump appears safer.

• 14 •

ACCURATE BIDDING FOR A SLAM

Auction Bidding

South	West	North	East
Pass	1 ♦	1 ♠	2 ♣
Pass	Pass	Pass	

Contract Bidding

South	West	North	East
Pass	1 ♦[1]	1 ♠	2 ♣[2]
2 ♥	3 ♥[3]	Pass	3 ♠[4]
Pass	6 ♣[5]	Pass	Pass
Pass			

Contract: 6 ♣ by Mrs Culbertson.
Result: Made six.
Lead: ♥ 7 by Mr Jacoby.

ANALYSIS OF CONTRACT BIDDING

[1] The longer of two biddable suits is shown first.

[2] Offering an alternative suit.

[3] With a hand containing 4 ½ honour-tricks and a partner able to respond, the bid of Three Hearts is a Slam try. It is justified because of the general strength of the hand and the strong support for partner's Take-out.

[4] Mrs Culbertson shows control of the first round of the other suit bid by our opponents.

[5] Justified by the distributional values disclosed in the bidding.

· 15 ·
OPENING TWO-BID

Auction Bidding

South	West	North	East
			Pass
Pass	1 N T	Pass	2 ♣
2 ♠	2 N T	Pass	Pass
Pass			

Contract Bidding

South	West	North	East
			Pass
Pass	2 ♦¹	Pass	3 ♣²
Pass	3 ♦³	Pass	3 N T⁴
Pass	6 ♣⁵	Pass	Pass
Pass			

Contract: 6 ♣ by Mrs Culbertson.
Result: Made six.
Lead: ♠ K by Mr Jacoby.

ANALYSIS OF CONTRACT BIDDING

¹ Hands with this distribution should not be opened with a Forcing bid of Two in a suit with less than 5 ½ honour-tricks.

² Showing the possession of a biddable suit and not less than 1 honour-trick in the hand.

³ Disclosing re-bid strength in the suit. The bidding must be kept open by both partners until a game contract is reached.

⁴ Denying any values not already shown.

⁵ The extremely strong hand and adequate support for the Club bid fully justify the Raise to Slam, even though partner has shown only a biddable suit and 1 honour-trick. Note that although I held all four Aces, No Trump was never bid or supported by me. Slam at No Trump cannot be made, while the Slam contract at Clubs is safe against any defence.

• 16 •

DOUBLE OF A ONE-BID FOR PENALTIES

Auction Bidding

South	West	North	East
	1 ♦	1 ♥	Double
Pass	Pass	Pass	

Contract Bidding

South	West	North	East
	1 ♦¹	1 ♥²	Double³
Pass	Pass	Pass	

Contract: 1 ♥ by Mr Lenz (doubled).
Result: Down four.
Lead: ♠ K by Mr Lightner.

ANALYSIS OF CONTRACT BIDDING

¹ An illustration of the Approach principle. One Diamond is a far more informative bid than One No Trump.

² This Overcall seems justified in view of the 2 ½ honour-trick opening. It will be noticed that if West bids One No Trump, North will pass.

³ A Penalty Double. Even though the contract is only One Heart, a set of 4 or 5 tricks does not seem unlikely.

• 17 •

Auction Bidding

South	West	North	East
			Pass
1 N T	Double	2 ♠	Pass
Pass	Double	Pass	3 ♣
Pass	3 ♥	Pass	4 ♣
Pass	Pass	Pass	

Contract Bidding

South	West	North	East
			Pass
1 N T	Double[1]	2 ♠	Pass[2]
Pass	Double[3]	Pass	3 ♣[4]
Pass	3 ♥[5]	Pass	4 ♣[6]
Pass	5 ♣[7]	Pass	Pass
Pass			

Contract: 5 ♣ by Mrs Culbertson.
Result: Made five.
Lead: ♠ A by Mr Jacoby.

ANALYSIS OF CONTRACT BIDDING

[1] A strong Take-out Double on a hand containing 3 honour-tricks and a long and strong biddable suit.

[2] Too weak to respond in view of North's intervening bid.

[3] Again requiring partner to bid.

[4] A forced response.

[5] Showing my strong suit.

[6] Indicating that the hand contains at least a five-card suit.

[7] The hand is so strong that game should be bid.

HANDS FROM THE FIRST WORLD BRIDGE OLYMPIC

SOLUTIONS

• 18 •

North and South should reach a contract of Four Spades, preferably by the following bidding:

South	West	North	East
1 ♠[1]	Pass	2 ♠	Pass
3 N T[2]	Pass	4 ♠[3]	Pass
Pass	Pass		

[1] The Approach principle. When a hand contains a biddable suit, even a four-card minor, the suit and not the No Trump should be preferred as an Opening bid.

² With a partner strong enough to respond at all, South should insist upon playing the hand at a game contract. The bid of Three No Trump offers the Responding Hand a choice as to the proper game declaration.

³ North's had would lose 1 trick in value if played at No Trump. There is also the added danger of two weak unstopped suits.

The play:

The play of this hand illustrates the following points:

1. Refusing to win the first lead of Diamonds, in order to prevent East from getting in the lead.

2. The lead of the 8 of clubs by South, in preference to the 2, in order to afford an additional entry to Dummy.

3. An elimination, or strip-play, by which West is thrown in the lead with the Queen of Hearts and is then unable to make any lead which will not lose him a trick.

(The card underlined takes the trick)

Trick	West	North	East	South
I	♦ Q	♦ 3	♦ 6	♦ 9¹
2	♦ J	♦ 7	♦ 4	♦ A
3	♣ 6	♣ A	♣ 9	♣ 8²
4	♠ K	♠ 9	♠ 4	♠ 5
5	♠ 2	♠ 3	♠ 6	♠ 10
6	♠ 8	♠ Q	♥ 2	♠ J
7	♣ 7	♣ 3	♣ 10	♣ J
8	♦ 2	♣ 4	♣ Q	♣ K
9	♦ 8	♣ 5	♦ 5	♣ 2³
10	♥ Q	♥ J	♥ 3	♥ 5
II	♥ 8	♥ 7	♥ 4	♥ 9
12	♥ K	♥ 10	♥ 6	♥ A
13	♦ 10	♠ 7	♦ K	♠ A

¹ South must refuse to win the first Diamond trick, otherwise East will be enabled to obtain the lead with the ♦ King and lead a Heart, which will defeat the end-play.

² South must lead the ♣ 8 instead of the 2, in order to obtain an

additional entry in Dummy with the ♣ 5 in case the Club suit breaks favourably.

[3] South now uses his last entry to Dummy and on the next trick plays the Knave of Hearts. When this play is made, South is sure of his four-odd against any location of the Heart honours, as when West obtains the lead he will be forced to make a lead which will be disastrous to him.

• 19 •

A Slam contract should be reached, preferably by the following bidding:

South	West	North	East
	1 ♠[1]	Pass	3 N T[2]
Pass	5 ♠[3]	Pass	6 ♠[4]
Pass	Pass	Pass	

[1] Although holding a powerful hand, a bid of more than one by West is not justified.

[2] East's bid of Three No Trump shows a powerful hand with all suits stopped and encourages West to try for a Slam if he holds substantial re-bid values.

3 By his bid of Five Spades, West shows his powerful six-card Spade and his 3 honour-tricks.

[4] With his two Aces and King of partner's suit, the Slam bid is obvious.

The play:

The Slam contract is fulfilled by means of a squeeze play, which is absolutely marked after a few leads. The Heart finesse should be avoided as it is unnecessary.

(The card underlined takes the trick)

Trick	North	East	South	West
1	♣ Q[1]	♣ 2	♣ 7	♣ K
2	♦ 9	♦ A	♦ 5	♦ 8[2]
3	♦ 2	♦ 4	♦ K	♠ 5
4	♠ 2	♠ 9	♠ 4	♠ A
5	♠ 3	♠ K[3]	♠ 8	♠ 6
6	♠ 3	♦ 6[4]	♥ 3	♠ 7
7	♠ 10	♣ 4	♥ 4	♠ Q

8	♦ 10	♣ 8	♣ 9[5]	♣ 3
9	♦ J	♣ A	♣ J	♣ 5
10	♥ 2	♥ 6	♥ 8	♥ A
11	♥ 7	♦ 7	♥ 9	♠ J[6]
12	♥ 10	♥ K	♥ Q	♥ 5
13	♦ Q	♥ J	♣ 10	♣ 6

[1] North opens his singleton against the Slam contract as a surprise lead. With his trickless hand, the best chance of defeating the contract appears to be to secure a ruff in Clubs. West wins the trick with the King and takes stock. With a 3–2 division of Clubs, the hand is a lay-down for six. Failing this, a further chance is offered by the Heart finesse. West, however, should play to avoid the Heart finesse, if possible, in the event that the Clubs do not break. There is a chance for this by a squeeze on both opposing hands in Clubs and Diamonds. If North opens differently, West's play will be along the same lines as indicated here.

[2] West, accordingly, immediately plays the Ace of Diamonds from Dummy and ruffs one Diamond in his own hand.

[3] West plays two rounds of trumps in order to discover whether there is any abnormal trump distribution.

[4] West ruffs the third Diamond in his own hand and discovers that South has no more of that suit.

[5] West must allow South to win this trick, otherwise when South later obtains the lead with a Club he will immediately take 2 Club tricks.

[6] When West plays this card he knows that the hand is won, for North must retain the winning Diamond and South must retain the winning Club; therefore, North and South must each hold one Heart and the ♥ Queen must fall.

· 20 ·

This is a hand illustrating competitive bidding.

The best bidding should go as follows:

South	West	North	East
	2 ♠[1]	Pass	3 ♠
4 ♦[2]	4 ♥	5 ♦[3]	Pass[4]
Pass	Double[5]	Pass	5 ♥[6]
6 ♦[7]	Pass	Pass	Double
Pass	Pass	Pass	

[1] West's solid holding in Spades, Hearts and Clubs justifies an Opening bid of two, even though he has only 5 honour-tricks and a four-card suit.

[2] South should defend. His partner is marked with one Spade at the most and possibly none, and must, therefore, in all probability, hold several Diamonds. A penalty of 900 points is, of course, conceivable, but very improbable.

[3] While North holds defence against the Heart contract, he has no guarantee that the hand will be played at that suit. It appears probable that East will return to Spades, against which he has little defence. He holds better support for partner than can be expected, and believes that whatever loss may be sustained will be well worth while. He, therefore, raises the Diamond bid immediately.

[4] While East, in view of West's Opening Forcing bid of two, has support for either bid, he fears that his partner may attempt a Slam, which might not be made, in case he gives a Raise now.

[5] On West's information, he cannot go further. He, therefore, elects to make a Penalty Double.

[6] East reasons that five Hearts or five Spades can possibly be made, but that North and South probably hold freak distributions, which will make the penalty they incur very small.

[7] South anticipates the defeat of his contract, but does not believe the loss suffered will be a severe one. The fact that East has supported Spades would indicate that he should not lose more than 2 tricks in that suit, and possibly only 1. He knows that he has not more than a single loser in Hearts and Clubs and partner's Raise makes it improbable that all of these tricks are to be lost. The probable limit of his losses is, therefore, 2 tricks, which is partially counterbalanced by the honours held.

• 21 •

This hand illustrates a shaded response to a bid of one and a Jump re-bid by the Opening bidder.

The bidding:

South	West	North	East
			1 ♠[1]
Pass	1 N T[2]	Pass	3 ♠[3]
Pass	4 ♠[4]	Pass	Pass
Pass			

[1] A bid of one is the best on this hand, as East's trump suit is not strong enough to justify a bid of three or four.

[2] Although West has a rather poor hand, he should not allow the bidding to die, but should make a negative response of One No Trump, as he holds very close to 1 ½ honour-tricks.

[3] When East knows that his partner has at least some slight strength, game appears very probable. He shows his powerful Spade suit and 4 honour-tricks by a Jump re-bid of Three Spades.

[4] Although West's One No Trump was a minimum, his three trumps and doubleton Club are of sufficient additional value to justify a Raise to four, in view of partner's strong bidding.

The play:

After ruffing the second round of Clubs, East finds that he has as possible losers one Heart and two Spades, in addition to the Club which he has already lost. In order to insure fulfilling his contract, therefore, he must make every effort to lose not more than 1 Spade trick. His best play, therefore, is not to finesse the Spade, but first to lay down the Ace and, in case no opposing honour falls, to enter the Dummy and lead a second Spade from that hand. This play insures losing not more than 1 Spade trick unless South holds K J 10. In this event, of course, 2 Spade tricks must be lost, no matter what play is made. As the cards lie, five-odd are made by the play of the Ace of Spades.

• 22 •

This hand illustrates a two-bid and proper responses by partner.

The bidding:

South	West	North	East
2 ♣[1]	Pass	2 N T[2]	Pass
3 ♠[3]	Pass	4 ♣[4]	Pass
5 ♣	Pass	Pass	Pass

[1] With 5 ½ honour-tricks and a semi-two-suited hand, South has an obvious Opening bid of two.

[2] With North's weak hand, the Two No Trump response is also obvious.

[3] South completes the showing of the distribution of his hand.

[4] North's obvious bid, with his 4-3-3-3 distribution, is a minimum response of Three No Trump. On closer consideration, however, it must appear that this bid is a sure loser. South's strength is obviously concentrated in three suits, two of which are Clubs and Spades; consequently, opponents must hold a solid suit of either Hearts or Diamonds. With the Queens of both of his partner's suits, a five Club contract appears safe.

The play:

The play of this hand illustrates an elimination, or strip-play.

(The card underlined takes the trick)

Trick	West	North	East	South
I	♥ K̲	♥ 2	♥ 8	♥ 4
2	♥ A̲	♥ 3	♥ 7	♣ 10
3	♣ 5	♣ 3	♣ 2	♣ A̲
4	♣ 8	♣ 9̲	♣ 7	♣ 6
5	♥ 6	♥ 5̲	♥ 10	♣ K
6	♠ 3	♠ 4	♠ 7	♠ K̲
7	♠ 6	♠ Q̲	♠ 8	♠ 2
8	♠ 9	♠ 5̲	♥ J	♠ A
9	♠ J	♣ 4	♥ Q	♠ 10̲
10	♦ K̲	♦ 10	♦ J	♦ Q
11	♦ 6	♦ 5	♦ 9	♦ A̲

South takes the rest of the tricks.

After ruffing the second Heart, South exhausts the trumps and eliminates the last Heart from Dummy by ruffing it in his own hand. When he finds that the Spade suit does not break, he ruffs the last Spade in Dummy and plays the ♦ 10. This play insures the loss of only one more trick, as when West obtains the lead any lead he may make will cost him a trick.

• 23 •

This hand illustrates a Grand Slam bid in Clubs by North and South and a Defensive Overcall of Seven Diamonds by East and West.

The bidding:

South	West	North	East
		1 ♣[1]	1 ♦
2 ♦[2]	Pass	3 ♣[3]	3 ♦[4]
6 ♣[5]	6 ♦[6]	7 ♣[7]	Pass
Pass	7 ♦[8]	Double	Pass
Pass	Pass		

[1] The best bid for North is a bid of One Club only.

[2] South shows no Diamond losers and a probable Slam.

[3] North shows a good Club suit on his re-bid; no need to hurry the bidding by a higher bid.

[4] East re-bids his Diamonds merely to show a possible defence.

[5] The Small Slam bid is obvious.

[6] West believes the penalty at Diamonds will cost less than a vulnerable Slam.

[7] North is absolutely assured of a Grand Slam. South, by his bidding, is positively marked with the Ace of Spades, the King of Hearts and a void in Diamonds.

[8] West feels sure that East holds no other strength than his powerful Diamond suit and that the adverse Grand Slam is assured. Consequently, he prefers to take a non-vulnerable penalty.

The play:

In the play at Diamonds this hand calls for good defence by North and South. South, on the fourth trick, must underlead his Ace-Knave of Spades for partner to ruff, retaining his tenace in that suit.

(The card underlined takes the trick)

Trick	South	West	North	East
1	♥ K[1]	♥ 3	♥ A[2]	♥ 5
2	♠ 9	♠ 3	♠ K	♠ 2
3	♥ J	♥ 4	♥ 6	♥ 7
4	♠ 8[3]	♠ 5	♦ 3	♠ 4

[1] South should open his King-Queen-Knave Heart combination in preference to Clubs, in which opponents probably are void.

[2] North overtakes his partner's Heart in order to lay down the singleton King of Spades.

[3] South places his partner with a singleton King, because he failed to continue the Spade after the encouraging play of the 9. Consequently, by leading his low Spade he can allow his partner to ruff and at the same time assure himself 2 more tricks in Spades with his Ace and Knave.

· 24 ·

This hand is the second illustration of a shaded response to an Opening bid and of a Forcing re-bid by the Opening Hand.

The play shows how a trump suit of nine cards headed by the A K Q should be played in the safest possible manner to avoid losing any tricks in that suit.

East—West par—Five Diamonds bid and made.

The bidding:

South	West	North	East
	I ♠[1]	Pass	I N T[2]
Pass[3]	3 ♦[4]	Pass	4 ♦[5]
Pass[6]	5 ♦[7]	Pass	Pass
Pass			

[1] West has a very powerful hand, but he is not justified in opening with a bid of more than one, for, if his partner is unable to make some response to a one-bid, game is impossible.

[2] Another example of a shaded response which must be made in order to give partner a chance to re-bid.

[3] Apparently South holds a perfectly legitimate Two Club Overcall, but against vulnerable opponents it is not advisable to overcall No Trump bids when in the lead. South hopes that East and West will get still higher in No Trump and enable him to lead his Clubs and probably defeat the contract. Against a suit bid South would obviously have bid Two Clubs.

[4] West now knows that partner holds some strength and consequently is determined that the hands shall be played at a game contract. He therefore bids Three Diamonds, a Forcing bid which compels partner to continue to game. It will be seen by this bid that

Forcing Take-outs are not restricted to the Responding Hand but can be used by either partner. West's hand is not strong enough to open with a Forcing bid, but, when he is assured that his partner holds some strength, he must make certain that the bidding will continue to game.

[5] East makes the only possible response. West is probably short in either Hearts or Clubs, and East has a stopper in neither of these suits.

[6] The bidding is now too high for South to speak. In this particular case it would probably have been better had he bid his Clubs immediately, but in the vast majority of hands passing tactics usually win, since the opponents are then not warned away from No Trump by showing the adverse suit held against them.

[7] West now bids for the game, confident that there is no Slam in the hand in view of East's minimum bidding.

• 25 •

This hand illustrates a game bid in Spades, as follows:

South	West	North	East
			1 ♠
Pass	3 ♠	Pass	4 ♠
Pass	Pass	Pass	

The play:

This had illustrates a difficult playing problem—a count of the opponents' hands by means of drawing every possible inference from opponents' leads and the fall of opponents' cards.

(The card underlined takes the trick)

Trick	South	West	North	East
1	♦ 2	♦ 9	<u>♦ K</u>	♦ 6
2	♦ 5	♦ Q	<u>♦ A</u>	♦ J
3	♥ 3	<u>♥ A</u>	♥ 10	♥ 4
4	♥ 6	♥ 7	♥ 2	<u>♥ Q</u>[1]

5	♥ J	♣ 2	♥ 5	♥ K
6	♠ 4	♠ 3	♠ 10	♠ K
7	♠ 5	♠ 6	♠ 3	♠ J

Declarer concedes 1 Club trick to opponents.

[1] South's Opening lead of the ♦ 2 evidently marks him with four Diamonds to the Ten as the highest possible card, the Ace-King-Queen-Knave being accounted for. Declarer has lost two Diamonds and must lose 1 trick in Clubs. Consequently, the making of his contract depends on capturing the ♠ Queen. Before determining how to play this suit, he decides to play three rounds of Hearts to see whether this will give him any further information as to the distribution of opponents' hands. There is no danger of an over-ruff by North in this play, because if South had six Hearts to the Knave he would prefer that as an Opening to four Diamonds to the Ten. When South drops the ♥ Knave on the third round, East can be reasonably sure that South held four Diamonds and three Hearts. South cannot have as many as four Clubs; otherwise he would have had a Club Opening which would have been much preferable to the Diamond lead. Consequently, South must hold at least three Spades. Declarer, therefore, plays his ♠ King, and when the Ten falls from North, finesses for the Queen on the second lead.

• 26 •

This hand illustrates competitive bidding and judgement as to how high to carry the bidding before doubling.

The bidding:

South	West	North	East
	1 ♥[1]	1 ♠[2]	4 ♥[3]
4 ♠[4]	Double	Pass	5 ♥[5]
Pass	Pass	5 ♠[6]	Pass
Pass	Double	Pass	Pass
Pass			

[1] West should prefer a bid of one in his higher-valued four-card suit to No Trump.

291

[2] North's hand is somewhat tempting for a Jump Over-call, but in view of the weakness of the Spade suit and the bare 2 ½ honour-tricks, a bid of one only is preferable.

[3] Although East's hand is somewhat weak in honour strength for this bid, the distribution and strong trump holding justify it. Then, too, it may result in shutting out opponents.

[4] South's Raise is somewhat shaky, but his hand is defenceless and the penalty at Spades may result in a saving.

[5] East's hand is practically trickless against a Spade declaration; consequently, he refuses to allow the Double to stand.

[6] From North's hand it appears not improbable that five Hearts can be made. A set of more than 2 on his hand is almost out of the question and there even appears a slight chance of fulfilling the contract.

The play:

This is an example of a hand where a trump lead should be deferred until late in the play.

(The card underlined takes the trick)

Trick	East	South	West	North
1	♥ A	♥ 4	♥ 6	♥ 5
2	♦ 3	♦ 2	♦ K	♦ A
3	♥ 2	♠ 4	♥ 10	♥ 7
4	♦ 8	♦ 6[1]	♦ 7	♦ Q
5	♦ J	♦ 10	♥ Q	♦ 4
6	♦ 9	♠ 7	♠ 10	♦ 5
7	♥ 8	♠ K	♠ Q	♠ 3
8	♣ 3	♣ 2	♣ 8	♠ 5
9	♣ 5	♣ 4	♠ J	♠ A

North takes the balance of the tricks.

[1] Declarer should not now lead trumps and hope for a favourable division of trumps or an even break in Diamonds. He should play two more rounds of Diamonds, preparing to ruff the fourth Diamond in Dummy in case the suit does not break evenly.

• 27 •

This is a Goulash deal (not passing). It illustrates the proper bidding of a thirteen-card suit and the drawing of the proper inferences by the opponents.

The bidding:

South	West	North	East
1 ♣	7 ♥ ?[1]	7 N T[2]	Pass
Pass	Pass		

[1] West should not bid his lay-down Grand Slam immediately, as it will be a warning to opponents of his probable holding and will tempt them to defend. From his hand a defensive bid of 7 ♠ is by no means improbable, so he should make some lower bid: or better still, pass.

[2] When West bid Seven Hearts vulnerable, North can make the definite inference that he has a thirteen-card Heart suit. South cannot have a trick in Hearts. On his Opening bid he is, therefore, definitely marked with the ♣ A, so if West had a card of any other suit in his hand, it must be a loser. As East can have none of his partner's suit to lead, the bid of Seven No Trump is safe. If West does not bid Seven Hearts immediately, it will be impossible for North to draw this inference, so he will eventually be forced to bid Seven Diamonds and to double the bid of Seven Hearts.

The play:

When West wins the first trick with the Heart Ace, it is apparent that Five Diamonds will be made unless all four trumps are held by North. A common error, made even by fine players, would be first to lead the King or the Queen from West. This play can gain nothing, since if the North hand holds the four outstanding trumps, a trick must be lost. On the other hand, if they are held by South, they may all be captured by the play of the Diamond Ace from Dummy, since the K Q 9 will be over the J 10 8. This is actually the situation in this hand, and West must play the Ace first in order to make his contract.

293

PROBLEMS OF PLAY AT CONTRACT BRIDGE

SOLUTIONS

• 28 •

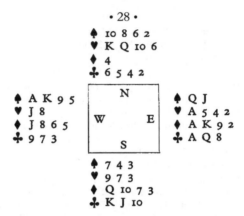

♠ 10 8 6 2
♥ K Q 10 6
♦ 4
♣ 6 5 4 2

♠ A K 9 5
♥ J 8
♦ J 8 6 5
♣ 9 7 3

♠ Q J
♥ A 5 4 2
♦ A K 9 2
♣ A Q 8

♠ 7 4 3
♥ 9 7 3
♦ Q 10 7 3
♣ K J 10

The point here is that Declarer can count nine tricks against any defence—Four Spades, Three Diamonds, One Heart and One Club—provided that he can make an entry in Dummy.

Hence he must play to the first trick the Ace or King of Diamonds. He then leads out his Queen and Knave of Spades, and plays, at trick 4, a small Diamond up to Dummy's Knave.

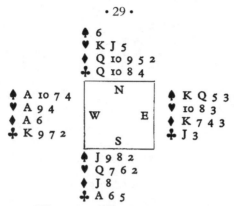

(*The card underlined takes the trick*)

Trick	North	East	South	West
I	♦ 5	♦ 3	♦ J	♦ A
2	♠ 6	♠ Q	♠ 2	♠ 4
3	♣ 4	♠ K	♠ 8	♠ 7
4	♥ 5	♠ 5	♠ 9	♠ 10
5	♦ 2	♠ 3	♠ J	♠ A
6	♣ Q	♣ 3	♣ 5	♣ 2
7	♦ Q	♦ K	♦ 8	♦ 6
8	♣ 8	♣ J	♣ 6	♣ K
9	♣ 10	♦ 4	♣ A	♣ 7
10	♥ J	♥ 3	♥ 2	♥ A
II	♦ 9	♦ 7	♥ 6	♣ 9
12	♥ K	♥ 8	♥ 7	♥ 4
13	♦ 10	♥ 10	♥ Q	♥ 9

West secured nine tricks.

Note: (1) how West sets up the Spade finesse in his own hand;

(2) at trick 6, the play of the small Club up to Dummy's Knave;

(3) the lead of the ♣ J at trick 8, overtaken by the King. It is essential Declarer should secure another round of the suit before losing the Ace of Hearts.

• 30 •

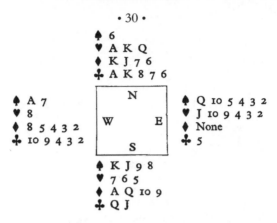

The hand illustrates how the adversaries' strength in trumps can be nullified by the setting-up of a cross-ruff:

(The card underlined takes the trick)

Trick	West	North	East	South
I	♠ 2	♠ 6	♥ 2	♠ <u>9</u>
2	♣ 2	♣ 6	♣ 5	<u>♣ Q</u>
3	♣ 3	♣ 7	♥ 3	<u>♣ J</u>
4	♥ 8	♥ A	♥ 4	♥ <u>5</u>
5	♣ 4	<u>♣ A</u>	♠ 2	♥ 6
6	♣ 9	<u>♣ K</u>	♠ 3	♥ 7
7	♠ <u>A</u>	♠ 6	♠ 4	♠ J
8	♦ 3	♦ 7	♥ 9	♦ <u>10</u>
9	♠ 7	♣ 8	♠ 5	♠ <u>K</u>
10	♣ 10	<u>♦ J</u>	♠ 10	♠ 9
11	♦ 4	♥ K	♥ 10	♦ <u>Q</u>
12	♦ 5	♦ K	♠ Q	♠ <u>8</u>
13	♦ 8	<u>♥ Q</u>	♥ J	♦ A

Note the Declarer's Spade finesse at trick 7, without which he cannot fulfil his contract.

• 31 •

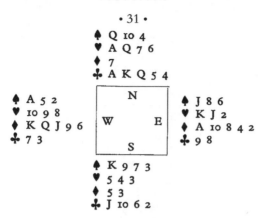

This hand was played in a championship match by Mr Gratz M. Scott, of the Cavendish Club of New York. "Mr Scott", says the *Bridge World*, "felt he was down one or two when he saw the Dummy. Desperate circumstances require desperate chances, and he resolved on them."

The hand as played:

(The card underlined takes the trick)

Trick	West	North	East	South
1	♦ **K**	♦ 7	♦ 8	♦ 3
2	♥ **10**	♥ Q	♥ K	♥ 3
3	♠ **A**	♠ 4	♠ 6	♠ 3
4	♥ 9	♥ **A**	♥ 6	♥ 4
5	♠ 2	♠ **Q**	♠ 8	♠ 7
6	♣ 3	♣ 4	♣ 8	♣ **10**
7	♦ 6	♠ **10**	♦ 2	♦ 5
8	♣ 7	♣ **5**	♣ 9	♣ J
9	♦ 5	♥ 6	♠ J	♠ **K**
10	♦ 9	♣ A	♦ 4	♣ **6**
11	♦ J	♣ **K**	♦ 10	♣ 2
12	♥ 8	♣ **Q**	♦ A	♥ 5
13	♦ Q	♥ 7	♥ J	♠ **9**

• 32 •

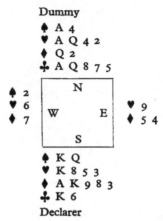

Dummy

♠ A 4
♥ A Q 4 2
♦ Q 2
♣ A Q 8 7 5

♠ 2   ♥ 9
♥ 6   ♦ 5 4
♦ 7

♠ K Q
♥ K 8 5 3
♦ A K 9 8 3
♣ K 6

Declarer

The ♥ 6 led is probably the bottom of a four-card suit, since the 5, 4, 3, 2 are all in sight. Hence, as West has only one Diamond, he presumably has three four-card suits, since a five-card suit would have been opened in preference to a four-card suit would have been opened in preference to a four-card one. Thus the adverse Clubs are distributed 4-2 and a long club trick can be set up at once. South will make his contract with four Club tricks, three Diamonds, three Hearts, and two Spades.

Lenz
- ♠ J 10 9 6 2
- ♥ Q
- ♦ 4 3
- ♣ Q 10 5 4 2

Culbertson
- ♠ A 7
- ♥ A J 3 2
- ♦ Q 10 2
- ♣ A J 7 3

N
W   E
S

Von Zedtwitz
- ♠ Q 4 3
- ♥ K 6 5 4
- ♦ A K 7 6 5
- ♣ K

Jacoby
- ♠ K 8 5
- ♥ 10 9 8 7
- ♦ J 9 8
- ♣ 9 8 6

This is a hand (No. 420) from the Culbertson–Lenz match.

The main points of play are:

(1) Declarer must not cover the ♥ 10 led with Dummy's Knave. If he does this he loses at once.

(2) A Heart trick being lost for certain, Declarer is faced also with the loss of a Spade. Von Zedtwitz brilliantly surmounted this difficulty by throwing the lead into South's hand at trick 11.

(*The card underlined takes the trick*)

Trick	South	West	North	East
1	♥ 10	♥ 2	♥ Q	♥ K
2	♣ 6	♣ 3	♣ 2	<u>♣ K</u>
3	♦ 8	<u>♦ Q</u>	♦ 3	♦ 5
4	♦ 9	♦ 2	♦ 4	♦ K
5	♦ J	♦ 10	♠ 2	<u>♦ A</u>

6	♥ 7	♥ J	♠ 6	♥ 6
7	♣ 8	♣ A	♣ 4	♠ 3
8	♣ 9	♣ 7	♣ 10	♦ 6
9	♥ 8	♥ A	♠ 9	♥ 5
10	♠ 5	♣ J	♣ Q	♦ 7
11	♥ 9	♥ 3	♣ 5	♥ 4
12	♠ 8	♠ 7	♠ 10	♠ Q
13	♠ K	♠ A	♠ J	♠ 4

PROBLEMS OF BIDDING AND PLAY AT CONTRACT WHIST

SOLUTIONS

• 34 •

Score: **Love-all. South deals**

```
           ♠ A Q 8 3
           ♥ 4 2
           ♦ 10 9 6
           ♣ Q J 9 2
```

♠ K 9 4   ♠ J 10 7 2
♥ A Q 10 7 6   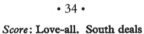   ♥ 9 8 5
♦ K 7 5   W   E   ♦ J 8 3 2
♣ 10 6   ♣ K 3

```
           ♠ 6 5
           ♥ K J 3
           ♦ A Q 4
           ♣ A 8 7 5 4
```

The bidding:

	South	West	North	East
South	1 ♣		2 N T	3 N T
West	1 ♥		No Bid	No Bid
North	1 ♠		3 ♣	No Bid
East	No Bid		No Bid	No Bid

Final contract: Three No Trump (South).

The play:

(The card underlined takes the trick)

Trick	West	North	East	South
1	♥ 7[1]	♥ 2	♥ 5	♥ J̲
2	♠ 4	♠ A̲[2]	♠ 2	♠ 6
3	♣ 6	♣̲ Q	♣ K	♣ A
4	♣ 10	♣̲ J	♣ 3	♣ 4
5	♦ 5	♣̲ 9[3]	♦ 2	♣ 5
6	♠ 9	♣̲ 2	♦ 3	♣ 7
7	♥ 6	♦ 6	♥ 8	♣̲ 8
8	♠ K	♠ 3	♠ 7	♠̲ 5[4]
9	♥̲ A	♥ 4	♥ 9	♥ 3
10	♥̲ Q	♦ 9	♠ 10	♥ K
11	♦ 7	♦ 10	♦ 8	♦̲ A
12	♦̲ K	♠ 8	♦ J	♦ 4
13	♥̲ 10	♠ Q	♠ J	♦ Q

Result: N—S make nine tricks and their contract.

NOTES ON HAND 34

[1] West leads his fourth-best Heart.

[2] North cannot finesse. If East holds the ♠ K he will lead through South's guard in Hearts.

[3] Unblocking South's suit.

[4] South can now read West's hand.

Score: Game-all. West deals

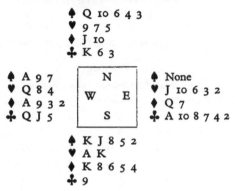

♠ Q 10 6 4 3
♥ 9 7 5
♦ J 10
♣ K 6 3

♠ A 9 7   N   ♠ None
♥ Q 8 4 W   E ♥ J 10 6 3 2
♦ A 9 3 2   ♦ Q 7
♣ Q J 5   S   ♣ A 10 8 7 4 2

♠ K J 8 5 2
♥ A K
♦ K 8 6 5 4
♣ 9

The bidding:

West	1 N T	No Bid	Double
North	No Bid	3 ♠	No Bid
East	2 ♣	4 ♣	No Bid
South	2 ♠	4 ♠	No Bid

Final contract: Four Spades (South) doubled by West.

The play:

(*The card underlined takes the trick*)

Trick	West	North	East	South
1	♠ A[1]	♠ 3	♥ 2	♠ 2
2	♠ 7[2]	♠ 4	♣ 2	♠ 8
3	♥ 4	♥ 5	♥ 3	♥ A
4	♥ 8	♥ 7	♥ 6	♥ K
5	♠ 9	♠ 10	♣ 4	♠ 5[3]
6	♦ A	♦ J	♦ Q	♦ K

7	♣ Q	♣ K	♣ A	♣ 9
8	♣ 5	♣ 3	♣ 10	♠ J
9	♦ 7	♦ 10	♦ 2	♦ 4
10	♥ Q	♥ 9	♥ 10	♠ K
11	♦ 9	♠ 6	♣ 7	♦ 8
12	♦ 3	♠ Q	♥ J	♦ 5
13	♣ J	♣ 6	♣ 8	♦ 6

Result: N—S are " set " one trick on their contract of Four Spades (doubled).

NOTES ON HAND 35

[1] West deduces from the bidding that his partner may have no trumps. Hence he leads the trump suit (cf. hand 4).

[2] West has diagnosed correctly. He continues the Spades.

[3] This continuation is poor. But it makes no difference, as West would lead the ♠ 9 on getting in with the ♦ Ace. The extraction of trumps by West defeats the contract.

· 36 ·

Score: Love-all. South deals

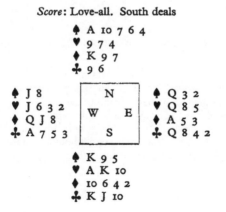

♠ A 10 7 6 4
♥ 9 7 4
♦ K 9 7
♣ 9 6

♠ J 8
♥ J 6 3 2
♦ Q J 8
♣ A 7 5 3

N
W   E
S

♠ Q 3 2
♥ Q 8 5
♦ A 5 3
♣ Q 8 4 2

♠ K 9 5
♥ A K 10
♦ 10 6 4 2
♣ K J 10

The bidding:

South	One No Trump
West	No Bid
North	No Bid
East	No Bid

Final contract: One No Trump (South).

The play:

(The card underlined takes the trick)

Trick	West	North	East	South
1	♣ 3	♣ 6	♣ Q	<u>♣ K</u>
2	♥ 2	♥ 4	♥ 5	<u>♥ K</u> [1]
3	♦ 8	♦ K	♦ A	♦ 2
4	<u>♣ A</u>	♣ 9	♣ 8 [2]	♣ 10
5	<u>♣ 7</u>	♦ 7	♣ 2	♣ J
6	♠ 8	♠ 7	♠ 2	<u>♠ K</u> [3]
7	<u>♠ J</u>	♠ 4 [4]	♠ 3	♠ 9
8	<u>♣ 5</u>	♥ 7	♣ 4	♥ 10
9	<u>♦ Q</u>	♦ 9	♦ 3	♦ 4
10	<u>♦ J</u>	♥ 9	♦ 5	♦ 6
11	♥ 3	♠ 6	♥ Q	<u>♥ A</u>
12	♥ 6	♠ 10	♥ 8	<u>♦ 10</u>
13	♥ J	<u>♠ A</u>	♠ Q	♠ 5

Result: N—S make their contract of One No Trump.

NOTES ON HAND 36

[1] To show North his certain entry, the ♥ Ace.

[2] East returns his highest remaining Club.

[3] If North has any strength, it is in this suit.

[4] North has "called". But he does not play his Ace. He has no card of entry, and takes a chance on South's holding a third Spade. The play is good, though it does not affect the result.

Score: N—S 3, E—W love, in the first game. West deals

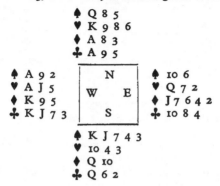

	♠ Q 8 5
	♥ K 9 8 6
	♦ A 8 3
	♣ A 9 5

♠ A 9 2   ♠ 10 6
♥ A J 5   ♥ Q 7 2
♦ K 9 5   ♦ J 7 6 4 2
♣ K J 7 3   ♣ 10 8 4

♠ K J 7 4 3
♥ 10 4 3
♦ Q 10
♣ Q 6 2

The bidding:

West	1 N T	No Bid
North	Double	No Bid
East	No Bid	No Bid
South	3 ♠	

Final contract: Three Spades (South).

The play:

(The card underlined takes the trick)

Trick	West	North	East	South
1	♠ 2[1]	♠ 5	♠ 10	♠ J
2	♠ A	♠ 8	♠ 6	♠ 3[2]
3	♠ 9[3]	♠ Q	♦ 2	♠ 4
4	♥ J	♥ 6	♥ 2	♥ 10
5	♥ A[4]	♥ 8	♥ 7	♥ 3
6	♥ 5	♥ K	♥ Q	♥ 4
7	♦ 5[5]	♥ 9	♦ 4	♦ 10
8	♦ 9	♦ A	♦ 6	♦ Q

9	♦ K	♦ 3	♦ 7	♠ 7
10	♣ 3	♣ A	♣ 4	♣ 2
11	♣ 7	♦ 8	♦ J	♠ K⁶
12	♣ J	♣ 5	♣ 8	♣ 6
13	♣ K	♣ 9	♣ 10	♣ Q

Result: N—S are "set" one trick on their contract of Three Spades.

NOTES ON HAND 37

The hand illustrates the resolute defence of tenace positions.

[1] West leads trumps for two reasons. He has a "tenace position" to defend in each plain suit, and it is possible that an adverse cross-ruff may develop. The lead of trumps may minimise its effectiveness.

[2] South's continuation of the trump suit suggests that he too is in a quandary.

[3] West continues his original plan.

[4] West still refuses to expose his ♦ and ♣ Kings. He can "cash" his ♥ Ace and get rid of the lead again.

[5] West must take a chance on East's holding the ♦ suit.

[6] The last trump! All is now well for E—W if South holds the ♣ Queen.

· 38 ·

Score: Love-all. East deals

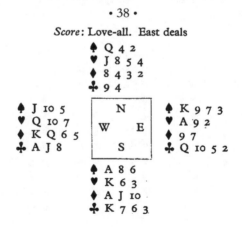

The bidding:

East	No Bid	No Bid
South	1 N T	No Bid
West	Double	
North	No Bid	

Final contract: One No Trump (South) doubled by West.

The play:

(The card underlined takes the trick)

Trick	West	North	East	South
1	♦ 5[1]	♦ 2	♦ 9	♦ 10
2	♣ 8	♣ 9	♣ 10	♣ 3
3	♦ Q	♦ 3	♦ 7	♦ J
4	♦ 6	♦ 4	♠ 3	♦ A
5	♠ 5	♠ Q	♠ K	♠ 6[2]
6	♣ J[3]	♣ 4	♣ 2	♣ 6
7	♦ K	♦ 8	♥ 2	♥ 3
8	♦ J[4]	♠ 2	♠ 7	♠ A
9	♣ A	♥ 4	♣ 5	♣ 7[5]
10	♠ 10	♠ 4	♠ 9	♠ 8
11	♥ Q	♥ 5	♥ A	♥ 6
12	♥ 7	♥ 8	♥ 9	♥ K
13	♥ 10	♥ J	♣ Q	♣ K

Result: N—S are "set" two tricks on their contract of One No Trump doubled.

The hand illustrates how the element of guesswork inevitably enters the play. At double dummy, the contract can be "set" four.

NOTES ON HAND 38

[1] West opens his four-card suit.

[2] South abandons the ♣ suit. This foreshadows the lead of Clubs by East which follows.

[3] West has no hesitation in finessing.

[4] West proceeds to establish a Spade trick; the defeat of the contract is in sight.

[5] South has inferred that West probably holds the ♣ Ace single.

• 39 •

Score: **Love-all.** North deals

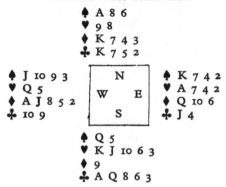

♠ A 8 6
♥ 9 8
♦ K 7 4 3
♣ K 7 5 2

♠ J 10 9 3   ♠ K 7 4 2
♥ Q 5   ♥ A 7 4 2
♦ A J 8 5 2   ♦ Q 10 6
♣ 10 9   ♣ J 4

♠ Q 5
♥ K J 10 6 3
♦ 9
♣ A Q 8 6 3

The bidding:

North	No Bid	1 N T	3 ♣	No Bid
East	No Bid	No Bid	No Bid	No Bid
South	1 ♥	2 ♣	4 ♣	
West	No Bid	No Bid	No Bid	

Final contract: Four Clubs (South).

The play:

(*The card underlined takes the trick*)

Trick	West	North	East	South
1	♠ J	♠ 6	<u>♠ K</u>	♠ 5
2	♠ 3[1]	♠ 8	♠ 7	<u>♠ Q</u>

3	♣ 9	♣ 2	♣ 4	♣ A[2]
4	♣ 10	♣ K	♣ J	♣ 6
5	♠ 9	♠ A[3]	♠ 2	♦ 9
6	♥ Q	♥ 9[4]	♥ 2	♥ 3
7	♦ A	♦ 3	♦ 6	♣ 3
8	♦ 2	♣ 5	♥ 4	♣ Q
9	♥ 5	♥ 8	♥ A[5]	♥ K
10	♦ 5	♦ 4	♦ Q	♣ 8
11	♦ 8	♦ 7	♥ 7	♥ J
12	♠ 10	♦ K	♠ 4	♥ 10
13	♦ J	♣ 7	♦ 10	♥ 6

Result: N—S make their Four Club contract.

NOTES ON HAND 39

[1] The ♠ Ace is clearly with North.

[2] South leads trumps. If North has the ♣ K he can lead out the ♠ A at trick 5 to give South a discard of his losing Diamond.

[3] Carrying out South's plan.

[4] Known to be South's second suit.

[5] South's Hearts are now established.

CHESS

• 1 •

1. Q—Kt 8, threatening 2. B—Q 5 mate.

• 2 •

1. Kt—Kt 7, waiting.

Twelve distinct mates accurately forced. The white K is an unfortunate necessity, as three extra pawns are needed to shield him.

• 3 •

1. R (B 1)—B 7, threatening 2. Kt—B 3 mate.

The well-known Kt-wheel problem. The black Kt creates eight variations, not one of which is dull.

• 4 •

1. K—B 7! threatening 2. Q—Q Kt 8 mate.

A fine early modern two-mover, with a bold key, inviting cross-checks from two directions, each showing "half-pinning" play.

• 5 •

1. Q—B 6! threatening 2. Q—Q K 8 mate.

The "half-pin" theme is again prominent in the main variations (1 … R—Kt 7 ch; 2. Kt—Kt 3 mate! and 1 … R—Kt 6 ch; 2. R—Kt 5 mate!). The black R's are said to be "half-pinned", as each by moving away leaves the other essentially pinned.

• 6 •

1. B—K 4! threatening 2. Kt x Kt mate.

"The standard cross-check problem of the twentieth century."
—A. C. White.

• 7 •

1. K—R 4! waiting.

There is no intricate strategy here, but the way in which the composer has restricted the key-piece to one square, with such slender forces, borders on the occult.

• 8 •

1. Q—B 1, threatening 2. Q—R 3 mate.

• 9 •

1. R—Q 7! (not Q 8), threatening 2. Q—KB 4 mate.

Although some purists may cavil at the dual (i.e. choice of mate) after purposeless moves of the black Q, this two-mover is unsurpassed for beauty of idea and execution. Note the three splendid unpins 1 … Q—Q 5,—K 4, and —R 1 ch (or—KB 7).

• 10 •

1. Q—K 7! threatening 2. R x Kt mate.

A ponderous affair redeemed by its galaxy of half-pins, with flight-giving key. White's diagonal battery opens in seven ways.

• 11 •

1. R—QB 2! threatening 2. Q—Q 7 mate.

The main variations are, of course, 1 …B x P; 2. R—B 6 mate (a switchback) and 1 … B x Kt; 2. R— Kt 2 mate (another self-pin).

• 12 •

1. Q—B 3!! threatening 2. Kt—Kt 4 mate.

Elegant construction emphasises the beauty of the key-move which liberates the doomed king and offers double sacrifice with a cross-check.

• 13 •

1. R—B 3, threatening 2. Q—R 4 ch! etc.
    if B x P;   2. P—B 3 ch, etc.
    if Kt x P;   2. R—Q 3 ch, etc.
    if B x R;   2. Q—R 1 ch, etc.

Each line leads to a pretty "model" mate. In a "model" no square around the vanquished king must be guarded superfluously and all the white men must assist in the mate with the permissible exception of the K and P's.

• 14 •

1. Kt—R 2, if P x KT; 2. Q—B 2, etc.
    if K—Q 7;   2. K—B 3, etc.
    if K—K 7;   2. Kt—Kt 4, etc.
    if K—Q 5;   2. B—B 2 ch, etc.

In an "echo" the same mating position is repeated on a different square, as in the first two variations given above.

• 15 •

1. P—Q 7, if P x P;   2. P becomes R.
    if P x B;   2. P becomes B.
    if K—Q 3;   2. P becomes Kt.
    if others;   2. P becomes Q.

• 16 •

1. Q—B 3! if Q x Q;   2. T x KtP, etc.
    if Kt x Q;   2. K x P, etc.
    if P x Q;   2. R x KP, etc.
    Threats: 2. Q—Q 3 ch, etc.
                  2. K x P, etc.

312

• 17 •

1. Kt—R 1! threatening Q—R 3, etc.
if R—Kt 6; 2. Q—B 1, R x Q (best); 3. Kt—B 2!
Etc., etc.

• 18 •

1. B—B 7, R—K 3; 2. R—R 8, R—K 6; 3. R—KB 8,
etc.

• 19 •

1. B—B 7, Kt x B; 2. R—Kt 8, R x R; 3. B—Kt 8, etc.
Kt—Kt 2; 2. R—Kt 8, R x R; 3. B x R, etc.

• 20 •

1. R—Kt! P—Q 6; 2. B—R 1, P—K 4; 3. R—Kt 2, etc.
P—K 4; 2. B—Q 8, P—Q 6; 3. B—Kt 6, etc.

• 21 •

Sam Lloyd, the former Puzzle King, wrote: "I made the
problem in 1858 at the Morphy Chess Rooms. It was quite
an impromptu to catch old Dennis Julien, the problemist,
with. He used to wager that he could analyse any position so
as to tell which piece the principal mate was accomplished
with. So I offered to make a problem which he was to analyse
and tell which piece did *not* give the mate. He at once
selected the Q Kt P as the most improbable piece, but the
solution will show you which of us paid for the dinner."

1. P—Q Kt 4 (threatening 2. R—Q 5 or KB 5), R—B 4
ch; 2. P x R (threatening 3. R—Kt 1 mate), P—R 7; 3. P—
B 6 (again threatening R—Q 5 or KB 5), B—B 2; 4. P x P,
any move; 5. P x Kt becomes Q mate!

• 22 •

1. B—K 5, B—R 8! 2. B x P! (otherwise 2 ... P—Kt 7 threatens stalemate). The white B then mates on the fifth move.

• 23 •

1. B—K 6, Q—R 4; 2. B—R 3, Q—K 4; 3. B—B 5, Q—K 1; 4. B—Kt 4, Q—K 4; 5. B—B 3, Q—K 1; 6. B—Q 5 and mates next move.

• 24 •

After the key-move (Q—Kt 1), which bottles up most of the hostile pieces, Black will naturally try to keep making non-committal moves with his Q R. To prevent this the W K will make his way to Q Kt 4. But how can he get there at the right moment and yet avoid dangerous checks by the black B? Here is the solution (abridged).

White's moves

1.	Q—Kt 1	32.	K—K 7
5.	K—K Kt 8	35.	K—Q Kt 4
10.	K—Q Kt 4	39.	K x P (Black's K B 5)
15.	K—K Kt 7	44.	K—Q R 8
20.	K—Q Kt 4	48.	K—Q Kt 4
24.	K—Q R 8	49.	K x R
29.	K—Q Kt 4	50.	Kt mates!!

Black's moves are omitted as his best plan is obvious. He will advance his pawns only when he cannot safely move his R.

Lloyd called it "The Walking Match".

LORD DUNSANY'S INFERENTIAL
PROBLEMS

• 1 •

1. Since the King and Queen are not on their own squares it is certain that they must have moved.

2. They cannot have moved without some of the Pawns moving.

3. Pawns cannot move backwards.

4. Therefore they must have come across the board from the other side.

The right-hand Kt then easily mates at Q 3 in four moves; or in three moves if Black adopts any other defence than 1 … Kt—K B 6 and 2 … Kt—K 4.

• 2 and 3 •

Answer: in A thus:

1. P x P e.p. B x R, or any move.

2. P to Kt 7 mate.

Black's last move can be proved to have been P (Kt 2) to Kt 4. There have been five captures made by Black, and four of them by Black's K P. The capture to spare cannot have been made by the Pawn at Kt 4 nor the Pawn at R 7 because a capture by either of them would have entailed coming out of, or going into, another Pawn's file, for which *two* captures would have been necessary. Also, had the Pawn at B 5 come there last time by capture from K 4, it must have taken him yet another capture to have got to K 4, because this is the file of the King's Pawn now at Q R 6. The Pawn at Q R 6 did not of course move last time from R 5, because he could never have got there. The Pawn at Kt 4 obviously did not move last time from Kt 3. The King could not have moved from in check of Knight and Rook at Kt 2 nor from the check of Pawn and Bishop at Kt 1.

315

But in "B", when the black Bishop is absent, the W P's may have made six captures (not seven as Black's Q B could never have moved), whereas in A the maximum is five. In A one capture is needed to get one of the Pawns into the K R file, and two captures to get another of them out of the way of the black Pawn in the K R file and then back again; for Black, having only one capture to spare, could not have got his Rook's Pawn round the white one: White's fourth capture is needed to get a Pawn to Q Kt 4. Now, with two captures to spare, as White has in diagram B, it is possible for White to have got his King's Pawn to K B 7 and, with another capture, to K 8. Thus Black *may* have had his King last time at Kt 2, and White's last move *may* have been P (B 7) x piece = Kt, double check, and the black King's last move may have been to R sq. While this possibility exists it is impossible to prove, as you can in A, that Black's last move must have been P (Kt 2) to Kt 4.

• 4 •

P x P e.p.

For no other move is possible for Black's last move than P (Q Kt 2) to Kt 4. The move of the Pawn from Kt 3 last time is of course impossible, as it would have been checking the white King before it moved. So would the Bishop, had it moved from B 2. And the black King cannot have moved from B 2, as its position there in check of the Knight and the Bishop would have been impossible. Equally impossible would have been its position at Kt 2, since it would there have been in check of a Pawn that could not have moved last time. The King's move last time from Q 4, in answer to a check from the white Pawn at K 4 capturing a piece, appears more probable; but it is impossible because that Pawn must then be the O B P and the Pawn at Q B 5 must then be the K B P, this arrangement demanding five captures. There are only six captures to spare, and three of these must go to the wanderings of White's K R P, which we will now come to.

Black appears to have been able to have moved last time one of two Pawns from K B 2; but this is impossible, because White's Bishop at B 3 must be a promotion, the original white K B not having been able to get out from his own diocese. He could certainly have got in and promoted at K 8 though there had been a black Pawn at K B 2, but he could never have got out again; consequently Black's K B 2 cannot have been occupied by any Pawn last time. Note that he could not have promoted on the white square at B 8, because his way is blocked now by the Pawn at Q 3, and must always have been blocked, because when this Pawn was not at Q 3 it must have been at Q B 2.

And a black Pawn could not have moved last time from K 2 because, if so, Black's Bishop could never have got out; and the Pawn could not have moved last time from Q B 2 because, if so, the Bishop could never have got in.

• 5 •

No. Because the board shows no other possible last move for Black than *Castles.* Therefore Black's King was, until Black's last move, at K sq. Now the King at K sq. does not prevent Black's Queen's Rook from having got out; but a King at K sq. with the power to castle is a previously immovable piece, and therefore Black's Queen's Rook could never have got out. It must therefore be a promotion. It could not have promoted at Q R 8, because, although Black has made a sufficient number of captures for his K P to have got to Q R 6 and thence to Q R 8, one of these captures is a white-going Bishop and not available for this journey; and it could not have got there via Q Kt 6, because that is occupied now by a Pawn, and when it was not occupied by that Pawn the road was then blocked by the Pawn at Q R 2. Black therefore must have promoted either at Q B 8, Q 8, K 8, K B 8, K Kt 8, or K R 8. The first four of these must have moved the King when the Pawn arrived at the seventh row or the eighth; and the last two, though possible without moving the white King on getting iǹ, must have moved either him or the King's Rook before the promoted black Rook got out.

· 6 ·

1. Kt to Q 6 +	1. P x Kt, or loses the Queen.
2. B to R 6	2. Q x B, or loses the Queen.
3. R to Kt 8 +	3. R x R, or mate next move.
4. Q to Kt 8 +	4. K x Q, *stale mate*.

THE
MANUSCRIPT
PAGES

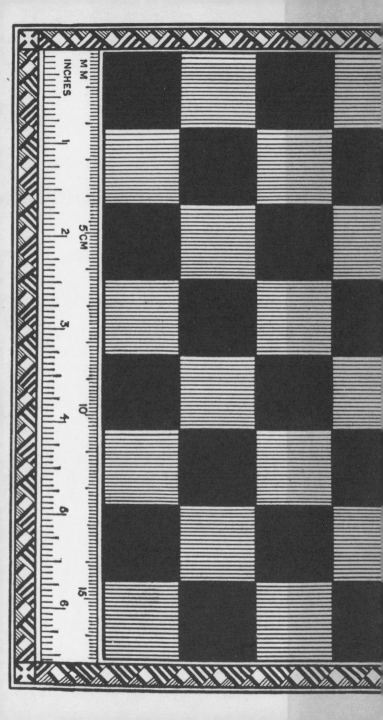